# THE HIDDEN MEANING OF PAY CONFLICT

Also by Michael White

MOTIVATING MANAGERS FINANCIALLY
INCENTIVE PAYMENT SYSTEMS FOR MANAGERS
SHORTER WORKING TIME

THE HIDDEN MEANING OF PAY CONFLICT

Michael White
Senior Fellow, Policy Studies Institute, and Research Associate, Ashridge Management College

© Michael White 1981

All rights reserved. No part of this publication may be reproduced or transmitted, in any form or by any means, without permission

First published 1981 by
THE MACMILLAN PRESS LTD
London and Basingstoke
Companies and representatives
throughout the world

ISBN 0 333 26833 4

Printed in Hong Kong

Contents

	Acknowledgements	vi
1	The Puzzle of Pay Conflict	1
2	Attitudes to Employment	13
3	Pay Attitudes and Pay Satisfaction	26
4	Pay Systems, Authority and Conflict	39
5	The Case-Survey Method	48
6	The Hotels	62
7	The Finance Company	79
8	The Manufacturing Plant	98
9	Summary and Implications	115
10	The Problem of Authority	131
	References	141
	Index	148

Acknowledgements

The research reported in this book involved interviews with 300 people, and the collection and analysis of 3200 questionnaires. Clearly this would not have been possible but for the help and co-operation of many people.

In the hotels study (Chapter 6), the field work was shared by Andrew Hepworth, Roger Hughes, Miranda Cummins and myself. The finance company field work (Chapter 7), was carried out by Roger Hughes, Tony Boyle and myself. The manufacturing plant field work (Chapter 8) was conducted by Andrew Hepworth, Bromwen Stiven and myself.

Andrew Hepworth worked closely with me on the planning and administration of the surveys, and many aspects of the exploratory investigations and survey procedures were discussed and decided jointly.

The multivariate statistical methods used in this research were selected on the basis of experience from a methodological study supported by a grant from the Social Science Research Council (Grant HR 2020, 'Systematic Analysis of Employee Satisfaction'). The team consisted of Peter Lansley, Roger Hughes and myself. Peter Lansley played the main role in this project, in terms both of statistics and of computer programming.

Particularly crucial was the support of the organisations from which the information was gathered. These three companies paid for the studies of their employees, yet gave every freedom to the researcher, and agreed that the work should serve research purposes as well as their own practical needs. Managers within the organisations contributed very substantially to the administration of the studies; and in two organisations support was also forthcoming from union representatives and officials. Above all, there were the individual employees who took part in the studies and created their substance.

The burden of typing the book has been carried by Janet Rabbetts.

I received much help and support from Professor Sylvia Shimmin, who supervised my doctoral thesis at the University of Lancaster,

Acknowledgements

from which this book developed. Professor Shimmin and Professor Hilde Behrend gave me encouragement to attempt this book, without which it would not have been written.

I gratefully record my appreciation to all these.

London
March 1979

MICHAEL WHITE

1 The Puzzle of Pay Conflict

Pay is a puzzle. But perhaps few people would see it like that. They would regard it as a commonplace aspect of everyday life. Everyone can feel that he knows about pay, just as everyone can be his own cinema critic. But if we do not find the workings of pay a perplexing topic, I suggest that it is time we did. For the problems of pay – the much-publicised disputes, recriminations and injustices – appear to be growing from year to year. How can we claim to understand it, when it is in such poor shape?

My personal curiosity about pay was aroused at an early stage of my work in industry – it was some years later that I began to study the subject and research it. The puzzling things I noticed in those early years were not so much the big strikes over pay (although there were one or two of those), but more the local frictions and emotional outbursts. For instance, when a new work planning system was being introduced, the people affected – maintenance engineers – were bitterly hostile towards any detail that affected the way their pay was to be calculated. This was even though the scheme offered them higher pay as a whole. Such a situation will be quite familiar to those who work in manufacturing industry: it is a common situation. Nevertheless, the hostile reactions aroused by such a situation need explanation. It is not transparently clear why changes in payment systems which offer higher earnings should sometimes arouse fervent opposition.

How do people involved in such situations interpret them? I seem to remember the term 'daft' being used frequently. 'You must be daft' said the shop stewards, or 'You must think we're daft if you think that we're going to "buy" this lot'. And the managers did think they were 'daft' – daft *not* to accept the scheme. It was a term to be muttered at the end of acrimonious meetings which had made no progress. But to cast aspersions on the sanity of the others is not an explanation of the situation. It is an admission that no explanation can be found; the situation is beyond reason.

And what are the reasons for this want of a reasonable explanation? It could be a convenient defensive stance. If the others are beyond reason, it's pointless to try to understand their problem or see their point of view. Or it could reflect a failure of a conventional way of looking at people's behaviour at work. The well-worn cliché, 'All they want is money', does not seem to fit the bill any more.

These occasions, when a new pay scheme offering more money is opposed, are not confined to manual workers. I myself have been a member of a 'professional' group of employees, which was offered a new salary structure with very considerable financial benefits. It created enormous tensions and hostility. By this time, I had worked out the theory which I describe in this book, and I accurately predicted the antagonism which the scheme would arouse. This did not prevent me from feeling as incensed as any of my colleagues.

I have started with anecdotes, but as will soon be apparent, there is a mass of more systematic evidence about these problems. The anecdotes should not and need not persuade anyone of the importance of the topic, but they do reveal my personal involvement with it. Although the method of this book is as detached and scientific as I can make it, I would not want to disguise that I still feel strongly about the problems of pay which I have experienced at first hand.

In fact, much of this book is about the *feelings* pay arouses – especially in those apparently inexhaustible conflicts around it. Any worthwhile explanation of conflict over pay must, I consider, be such as to make sense of the emotions we experience in these situations. Moreover, the explanation should not depend on a narrow concentration on the big and visible pay disputes where workers are battling for major pay increases. It should cope with the everyday, small-scale, half-veiled conflict over pay – which many people would not even call 'conflict', but is no less keenly felt and no less corrosive in its effects. It is from this category that my earlier anecdotes come, and it is this type of conflict which is most widely experienced in industry.

DIMENSIONS OF THE PROBLEM

For a start, we need some impression of the extent and the pervasiveness of conflict over pay. And to help in getting this, a preliminary distinction is useful. It is this: conflict occurs not only over *how much*

The Puzzle of Pay Conflict 3

one is paid, but also over *how* one is paid. It is not just the money in the pay packet which matters; the pay method which determines that money is itself a serious source of conflict, or at least an important contributing factor.

This is not by any means a new distinction. That founder of scientific management, Taylor, writing at the turn of the century, could already draw upon many examples of conflict over pay methods, and he himself saw a connection between these and wider non-monetary problems between management and workers. And from the 1930s onwards, there has been a steady stream of carefully observed case-study research, in both America and Britain, which reveals the significance of pay methods in the particular situations of conflict which were studied. Some of these, like the 'Hawthorne' studies[1], or the work of Donald Roy[2] and Tom Lupton[3] in observing shop-floor life at first hand, are generally regarded as among the classics of management research.

But if this was all that one had to go by, one could not be sure that one was not merely collecting special and peculiar cases. And if that were so, then the anecdotes with which I started this chapter, or the case studies which appear later in this book, could themselves be dismissed as further curiosities. But there is other evidence to show how massive the conflict over pay methods is, and has long been.

Consider as an example the history of strikes in the coal-mining industry. These, over the decades, have formed a very substantial proportion of all the strikes in Britain – until, that is, the 1960s when their number dramatically came down. The reason for this decrease is almost certainly the elimination of local pit-based incentive schemes[4]. And it is equally certain that a major factor in the enormous numbers of coal-mining strikes in the 1950s was those same pit-based incentive schemes.

Fresher and more direct evidence comes from a survey of wage determination in manufacturing industry, carried out in 1975 by W. W. Daniel[5]. The period of this investigation was a particularly 'quiet' one for industrial relations in Britain. Yet a quarter of the 250 manufacturing establishments surveyed had had industrial action in the previous year; this includes overtime bans, work-to-rules, and other actions less severe than strikes. About half had experienced situations where action had been *threatened* against the company. There is certainly much more conflict in industry than the official strike statistics reveal. Also, by directly questioning this cross-section of manufacturing industry about their disputes, Daniel showed that payment methods were not a subsidiary but a dominant factor in them. The *majority* of all these cases of industrial action taking place or being threatened were associated with problems concerning various types of 'payment by results' system.

There is yet another type of evidence. Between 1969 and 1975, there existed the Commission on Industrial Relations (CIR), among whose duties was to study and report upon companies suffering from a high level of industrial strife or unrest. It has subsequently been replaced by the Advisory Conciliation and Arbitration Service (ACAS), which has rather different statutory duties but continues to investigate deteriorating industrial situations. No systematic summary of the reports of these two bodies has yet appeared. But to anyone accustomed to reading or referring to them, it will be well known how frequently the theme of 'payment methods' recurs. Conflict around payment methods has continually been identified as an important component of deteriorating industrial relations.

Yet all these types of evidence taken together only cover the more conspicuous part of the problem. Strikes are widely acknowledged to be the tip of an iceberg; the CIR and ACAS have investigated companies where the problems are already reasonably serious; and Daniel's study, the most representative to date, considers nothing less substantial than an explicit threat of action. If one also took account of cases where employees felt aggrieved but threatened no action, for instance because they were too weak or unorganised, or if one considered situations where confused fears and mistrust were prevalent, but without materialising into solid grievances, then the problems of payment methods would surely be even more widespread.

It seems likely, then, that the situations I described in my two opening anecdotes are far from being curiosities, for they too covered pay methods rather than pay levels. If one appreciates the dimensions of the conflict over pay methods, then one may doubt whether pay conflict can in general be reduced to straight money terms. Conflict over pay *methods* can occur even where people stand to be better off as a result of the changes they oppose. But if money is *not* the general explanation, what is this *other* thing which arouses people to conflict?

SOME ATTEMPTS AT EXPLANATION

However, before I can justify developing my own explanation for pay conflict, I must give a fair hearing to established modes of explana-

The Puzzle of Pay Conflict

tion. I am referring not to explanations circulating in everyday speech, but to the more formalised explanations put forward by writers on industry. For instance, I have questioned the popular view that pay conflict is 'about getting more money'. But economists, or other writers with an economics approach, are not so lightly dismissed. Modern economic thought has proved surprisingly flexible in explaining observations which at first looked outside its scope.

This for instance was the approach used by Lupton – in the study referred to earlier – when he examined the behaviour of men paid on an incentive system. These men 'fiddled' the recording procedures of the payment system, and so regulated their earnings to a stable figure, rather than going all-out for maximum earnings. Lupton's analysis showed that the forgoing of economic gain was only superficial. In the first place, the men's strategy achieved consistent rather than fluctuating earnings, and this predictability in itself has an economic value. Also, calculations and comparisons suggested that the money forgone over a period was quite trivial, and certainly insignificant compared with the benefit of a more relaxed working life.

So the economic approach is not to be despised, and, in some respects, I am going to lean heavily upon it. The distinction between the economic and non-economic aspects of work behaviour is a complex one, which I will have to return to continually in later chapters. For the moment, I shall look at the economic type of explanation in a relatively superficial way: is there evidence which reduces its plausibility as an underlying source of conflicts over pay?

Apart from the anecdotal examples which I have already quoted, I think there is. Managers with experience in virtually any industry will be aware, for instance, that the groups most likely to engage in disputes over pay are the higher-paid manual workers. This is not merely an impression; it has been confirmed by a wide-ranging review of the evidence[6]. The low-paid groups, who one might suppose have the greatest economic reason for taking action, have also in general been the least active.

A similar picture is presented if one compares industries. A recent Department of Employment publication on strikes[7] confirms in detail what has long been known in general terms: the great bulk of strikes occur in a few industry sectors, and these are generally among the highest-paying. They include docks, coal-mining and vehicle manufacture. If a high material standard of life was the objective towards which pay conflict was driving, why do so many of the lowest-paying industries have a virtually strike-free record? Or if the relatively high pay of workers in mining or car assembly has been the result, not the cause, of a militant tradition, why have workers in other industries been so slow to emulate them?

Another statistical point, again from the Department of Employment's study, is that strikes are associated with periods of relatively rapid *increases* in pay. The same picture comes from Daniel's national survey: it is when a firm's demand is rising, when the order book is full, when recruitment rather than redundancy is taking place, that workers will more probably resort to industrial action. In short, it is when groups of workers are being more, rather than less, successful in economic terms, that they are most likely to strike.

Although evidence of this type is not totally incompatible with economic explanations of work conflict, it certainly makes the task more complicated. In any case, there has not been much steam behind a purely economic view of pay problems in recent years. Much more popular has been talk of 'differentials', 'relativities', and 'felt-fairness': it is such processes of comparison, using some kind of possibly non-economic criteria, which are often said to underlie the problems of pay. So it is argued, for example, that the low-paid are little involved in conflict over pay because they compare their position in a very limited way with others equally badly off, whereas the more militant high-paid groups are egged on by the wider comparisons they draw. So familiar is the talk of 'differentials' and 'comparabilities' in newspapers and parliamentary reports, that it is unnecessary to labour this point.

I make no bones about it: for all its popularity, this idea is so weak as to be logically questionable. Its logic will be probed in Chapter 3. For the moment, though, explanations are being assessed in terms of factual evidence, and the plausibility or implausibility which evidence confers. The notion of 'differentials' does not do well on this score, certainly not for an explanation so widely advocated.

Consider the large-scale surveys conducted by Hilde Behrend and her colleagues, at various times from 1966 to 1974, in both the United Kingdom and the Republic of Ireland[8]. The main theme of these surveys was the public's awareness of inflation, and the way in which their hopes and expectations about pay changed in an inflationary period. Summing up a great deal of this work, Behrend said: 'The findings suggest that the cost of living is by far the most frequently used reference frame . . . the adequacy of a pay increase amount (and by implication its fairness) is judged by the visibility of the benefits which it bestows – whether it enables the individual to keep up with inflation, to maintain or improve his standard of living, or is so small or arrives so late that it is considered valueless.' In this comment differentials are conspicuous by their absence. Behrend finds *some* significance in differentials, as one can see at other points of her discussion, but only in a minor and secondary way.

TABLE 1.1. Reasons for Considering that a Pay Increase is Fair

The data below have been reproduced from a study by Behrend* (see text for further details). It will be seen that reasons relating to the cost of living predominate, while reasons referring to comparisons between groups of workers comprise at most 15 per cent of the replies.

Reason	No. of Respondents	% of Respondents
It is needed to keep pace with the rising cost of living, to maintain the present standard of living.	168	36
Cost of living has increased.	133	28
Everyone should get the same/everyone has to pay the same extra costs.	38	8
It is the minimum that would make any difference.	35	7
The lower paid should get more than the higher paid/should get at least this.	29	6
It would help to curb inflation/would hold down the cost of living.	19	4
It would be reasonable provided prices (costs) are stabilised.	10	2
Higher paid people with more responsible jobs should get more.	4	1
Other reasons, don't know, no answer.	38	8
TOTAL	474	100%

SOURCE:
Behrend, H., Incomes Policy, Equity and Pay Increase Differentials (Scottish Academic Press, Edinburgh, 1973) p. 25.

Table 1.1 is reproduced from one of Behrend's survey reports. It states the reasons, spontaneously given by a cross-section of the working population, for assessing a pay increase as fair. Eight per cent were directly *anti*-differentials saying that 'everyone should get the same' or words to that effect; 6 per cent wanted differentials *reduced* rather than increased ('the lower paid should get more'); and just 1 per cent (4 individuals out of 474) said 'higher paid people with more responsible jobs should get more'.

None of the remaining remarks could be interpreted as having anything to do with differentials – mostly, they were about the cost of living, or the standard of living. So *only 15 per cent* were inclined to think spontaneously about differentials as something significant.

But even though differentials are not generally a focus of attention, they might be an important source of conflict when they *are* salient. The analyses of strike statistics, and the survey by Daniel, both of which I have already used, are once again the appropriate places to turn to for an answer. First, the study of strike statistics has yielded various analyses of the *reasons given* for strikes. Such reasons originate from the employers involved, from conciliation officers' reports, and from reports in the press: all these are classified as a matter of routine by Department of Employment officers. The statistics for 1966-76 showed that 56 per cent of all stoppages, and 82 per cent of all working days lost through stoppages, arose for reasons to do with pay. Of these, 3 per cent of stoppages and 5 per cent of working days lost were classified as due to 'pay parity issues'; 7 per cent of stoppages, and 5 per cent of working days lost, were due to 'pay differentials'. A total of *only 10 per cent* of the conflicts over pay is obtained on either score.

Daniel, in his 1975 survey of manufacturing industry, analysed the issues leading to industrial action, including less drastic actions than strikes, and also to threats of industrial action. He therefore came much closer to the everyday, grass-roots level in which I am primarily interested. Of the surveyed establishments which had industrial trouble in that year, he classified *20 per cent* as to do with 'comparability': 8 per cent were 'job grading/job evaluation' issues, and 12 per cent 'differentials/pay of one group relative to others'. At a later stage, I will present reasons for thinking that problems of job grading and job evaluation can be of quite a different character from problems of differentials. For the moment, though, accepting that all should be put under one heading, one still has the modest total of 20 per cent. Although this is the highest result of the three studies (the others were 10 per cent and 15 per cent), it is still hardly grounds for saying that differentials or comparability are the basic explanation of pay conflict.

In spite of this evidence from large and representative studies, some

The Puzzle of Pay Conflict 9

readers may still feel affronted by the suggestion that differentials are perhaps a minor, but not the major factor in pay conflict. Such a well established idea is not easily pushed aside by mere facts! It may help to consider, therefore, some of the *misleading evidence* which could help to explain the sacred awe in which the doctrine of differentials is held.

One source of misinformation is accounts of major strikes in newspapers and on radio and television. Since the doctrine of differentials appears well established in the news media, this aspect is very often seized upon and emphasised. An example is the coal miners' strikes of 1971/72 and 1973/74, the latter of which contributed to the 'three-day working week' and the fall of the Heath Government, and was therefore perhaps the most publicly conspicuous of post-war strikes. The media continually represented the strikes in terms of the miners being determined to 'climb back to the top of the pay league', but an historical analysis by Hawkins[9] led him to completely different conclusions. He emphasised the effect of Government intervention in public sector pay disputes, and the resulting shifts of power in negotiations, on the mineworkers changing their strategy from co-operation to conflict.

Another source of distorted perception, for those involved in negotiations or live conflict situations, is the sheer difficulty of differentials problems, when they arise. To quote Daniel's survey again, 43 per cent of managers found that comparability was the most *difficult* problem over pay, and 38 per cent thought of it as an issue giving rise to day-to-day claims. Yet only 18 per cent of managers found it a serious source of actual conflict (this ties in with the earlier quoted figure of 20 per cent, which was obtained by analysing *examples* of conflict). And finally, only 8 per cent of shop stewards found it a serious source of actual conflict. Managers become highly sensitive to differentials problems, because they are difficult to resolve, expose weaknesses and anomalies in the supposedly rational thinking behind pay structures, and are particularly well exploited by union officers and representatives.

As for the reason why the issue is so well exploited from the union side, long practice and familiarity is part of it; another part is the vulnerability of managers to this type of argument, because of their own personal values. It is well established that white-collar workers 'believe in' differentials more than do manual workers; managers more than non-managers; senior managers more than junior or middle managers. It is particularly awkward for managers to fend off arguments based on differentials, when their personal level of reward and status depends so much on the principle. Experienced union negotiators are naturally well aware of this.

So the evidence and arguments I have been putting forward in no way deny the importance of differentials from a negotiating viewpoint. The puzzle I am concerned with is the source and meaning of conflicts over pay, not the tactics of the negotiating table. I am searching for an explanation which, among other things, accords with the intensity of individual feelings aroused by pay issues even in situations which never approach outright industrial action. So the relatively lower level of sensitivity to differentials issues, in the population at large makes differentials an implausible type of explanation. That leaves room for another approach.

THEORY BUILDING

Having considered the explanations of pay conflict already available, and finding them unsatisfying, I can now introduce my own. The method I will use in this book is scientifically speaking a conventional one. I will build up a general theory about the reactions of employees to pay; then I will test that theory with data. The theory will generate a string of predictions about what the data should show. If the results do not fit the predictions, then the theory is best forgotten. But if the results are consistent with the theory, it should be kept and subjected by others to further testing – especially the acid test of putting it into practice.

This is textbook stuff, but it may appear unusual because it has not normally been applied to pay. Whole books of analysis, problem diagnosis and prescription are written without a theory ever being stated. When theories are presented, clear tests are not defined and systematic test data are not assembled. Above all, personal opinions or beliefs are held irrespective of the evidence. Pay dogma abounds. In attempting a theory-testing approach, I realise that I am assuming a respect for evidence which in this field does not generally exist. However, the only way to displace unscientific method is by proposing and demonstrating scientific method. Moreover, I believe, and hope to show, that the effort devoted to building theories pays off provided the theories are tested and do not remain mere speculation. Testable theories have practical implications.

The development of the theory presented here was a slow process occupying several years, during which evidence was being assembled. I wish that the outcome was something extremely simple, but it is not.

The Puzzle of Pay Conflict 11

The theory has three distinct parts, or sub-theories. To put it another way, the puzzle of pay eventually comes apart into three interlocking aspects. Only when one sees how and why the three parts fit together, can the puzzle be finally understood. It will probably be helpful to take a brief look at the complete approach before presenting each aspect in detail in the subsequent chapters.

The first and most unconventional step was to suppose that pay was *not* all of a piece. Instead, it could have different aspects, which people could react to in quite separate ways. To make this principle clear, let us imagine that theré are two aspects which we call 'Pay-1' and 'Pay-2'. A person can look at his pay from viewpoint 1 and feel happy about it; the same person can look at his pay from viewpoint 2 and feel unhappy about it. This could be possible, for instance, if adopting one viewpoint makes people notice only *some* details about pay, while adopting another viewpoint makes them pay attention to some *other* details.

This idea would – in principle – enable an explanation of those puzzling observations with which this chapter started. If people are fiercely opposed to certain pay methods, even when their adoption offers more money, it could be because those particular situations make them keenly aware of pay methods, for reasons other than money. But they could also rapidly shift their point of view and look at their pay in simple money terms. There is no need for us to suppose that they are not 'money-conscious'.

To take this idea further, I have to specify what these different viewpoints might be. What I argue in this book is that people *evaluate* their pay, and make up their minds whether they are satisfied or dissatisfied with it, on *economic* grounds. Although in fact people's perceptions of economic factors are much wider than they are usually given credit for, this 'economic' viewpoint on pay is reasonably close to the common-sense view of what pay is about. But *conflict* over pay cannot be explained in the same way. It is to do with action, rather than evaluation, and from this fact alone one can expect the thought processes and attitudes involved to be different. Perhaps that is a rather subtle distinction of psychology. But I argue that there is a much more solid and striking difference involved. I argue that, in fact, *conflict over pay is not directly concerned with economic issues, but with issues of authority and power.* Thus, I maintain, whether or not people are economically satisfied with their pay has no bearing on whether or not they are aroused to action. If one wishes to understand or predict conflict over pay, one must first of all understand the relationships of authority and power between management and workers, or among other groups involved in a situation. It is these which provide the conditions for conflict.

Conflict, authority, power: these are terms which people in industry find embarrassing and prefer to avoid. I will be giving a great deal of attention to explaining and illustrating their importance, at a later stage. For the present I ask the reader to suspend judgement and not to leap to any hasty conclusions about the sense in which these concepts should be interpreted. Nevertheless, let me suggest one link with points made previously. I have stressed that a great deal of pay conflict concerns pay methods: and are not pay methods one of the means by which management exerts its authority and controls the behaviour of workers? So, when workers aim to undermine that authority and resist that control, a natural result is conflict over pay.

Two strands of the puzzle have now been indicated, but there is still the third. For although these two aspects of pay may be logically quite distinct, there is still the question of how they coexist inside an individual, and how that individual switches from one viewpoint to the other. This is to do with individual psychology, especially the psychology of attitudes. Existing theories of attitudes to employment have not been developed to answer questions like these. I will put forward a theory in the next chapter, describing *structures* of attitudes which accommodate different perceptions of pay or other aspects of employment. But I will show that this idea of a complex attitude structure can be built up from a few simpler findings from psychology. The theory covers attitudes to all aspects of working life, not only pay, and this is useful for my purposes because it enables links between pay attitudes and other attitudes to be examined.

It has seemed best to put the psychological theory first, before the discussion of the 'economic' and 'authority' aspects of pay, because it provides a general framework into which the other elements can be slotted. It serves another purpose, too. The evidence for testing the theories is in the form of case studies, together with attitude surveys of employees, in situations of potential or actual conflict. The psychological theory provides an approach for testing the main ideas about pay in quite a direct manner, using the attitude survey information, rather than having to rely wholly on personal impressions and subjective interpretation. The psychological theory is the 'cement' which will hold together the ideas on how people react to pay and the evidence assembled to test those ideas.

2 Attitudes to Employment

To study attitudes to employment, it is usual to ask people series of questions, by interviewing them or by getting them to complete questionnaires. Then one has to interpret their replies. There are two basic issues to be faced in order to do this thoroughly. First, what is the nature of the replies – what are they about? And what are the relationships between the many answers to the different questions – what is their structure? By dealing with these issues at the outset, I hope to give a firm foundation to the remainder of the inquiry. That is the purpose of this chapter.

The method to be used in this chapter is psychological. But psychology is not a unified science; there are many competing schools of thought within it. The method I adopt is rather different from the bulk of psychological work on employment attitudes. It is derived from the 'cognitive' school of experimental psychology, and is also related to recent work in the psychology of consumer behaviour. It may help to clarify my approach if I first say something about the prevailing views of employment attitudes, explaining why I differ from them.

THE CONTENT OF EMPLOYMENT ATTITUDES

Psychologists who have studied employment, and employees' attitudes, have for the most part used a motivational approach, and especially the type of motivation theory which originally stemmed from psychoanalysis. This is true, for instance, of two writers who have had a great influence on management: McGregor[1] and Herzberg[2]; both writers draw on the theories of Maslow[3], who in turn acknowledges the influence of Freud and Adler. Motivational approaches of this kind are based on the notion that people have intrinsic *needs*, which they strive to satisfy through their various activities, including work. Employment is 'satisfying' to the extent that it fulfils these needs –

the entire topic is often referred to as 'job satisfaction' in this school of thought. It is also assumed by these writers that everyone has more or less the same needs, although their strength or intensity may vary.

The approach has an attractive simplicity about it. By asking people about how far they are satisfied with various aspects of their work, one seems to be gathering information which can be directly interpreted through motivation theory. It is true that Maslow warned against identifying superficial aspects of behaviour with deep motivations, but in practice this is often done. So 'job satisfaction' is analysed into 'components of satisfaction' such as pay, promotion, working conditions, and so on[4]. This simplification of people's work experience into a brief list is only possible because of the strong assumptions introduced at the outset: that employment attitudes are 'about' needs and need satisfaction, and that the needs are standard and unchanging from one social setting to another. Is it reasonable to make these assumptions?

There are many comments which people make about their employment which do not seem to be about needs in the psychological sense. If for instance someone says, 'This company is run very efficiently', he does not necessarily have any personal need to which that comment refers. It is about the situation in the company, not about his own state of need satisfaction. One can accept it as useful evidence about the company, and about his attitude to the company, by taking the comment entirely at face value. Again, if someone says, 'I think we should have a union here', that is a significant view which is not easy to pin down in terms of need satisfaction. It *might* be connected to various needs which the individual feels, but that would have to be found out separately – it is not a part of the comment itself.

In fact, if one looks at the questionnaires that 'job satisfaction' theorists have developed, one is struck by their narrow scope. By confining themselves to material which can be directly handled in terms of needs and satisfactions, they have excluded many facets of life at work, and of the views of working people, which cannot be reduced to those terms. There is much to be gained, in my view, by being open to the diversity of ways in which people speak about their work.

The assumption that human needs can be reduced to standard, universal categories also seems dubious. In the case of physical needs such as the need for food or warmth, it makes reasonable sense to suppose that those needs exist whoever the individual, and whatever the society in which he lives. But it does not seem so reasonable to suppose that this is true of more complex needs, such as some of those

Attitudes to Employment 15

which might be involved in attitudes to employment. Ambition and the desire for self-advancement are thought commendable in some societies, but pathological in others. Some people want to work in a progressive, innovative atmosphere, but by no means all. There is also little doubt that this kind of need has become much more common in industrialised societies than in older, rural communities. Examples of this sort suggest that needs vary both among individuals and between societies.

These more complex – social rather than physiological – needs are often what sociologists would prefer to call 'values'. To speak of needs suggests something wholly inside the individual, whereas to speak of values affirms the social dimensions of experience. The urge to innovate may belong to relatively few people, but values directly or indirectly connected with innovation are widespread. Others can understand the innovator's efforts, even when they do not share his priorities. Values support and shape the innovator, giving him a 'place in society'. But societies where the *idea* of innovation has not become established will regard the man who tries to innovate as ill or unfortunate.

Having objected to the notion of standard, unchanging needs, I am not going to put values in their place. Values have been mentioned as an *illustration* of the way in which individual experiences of work are shaped by interpretations learned from others. But there are many ways in which employment can be talked about, without necessarily expressing values. There are hopes, beliefs, descriptions, intentions, speculations, preferences, and many other types of expression. Some may involve values, others not. Moreover, the meanings of language may change more rapidly than values (or needs for that matter). Concepts are reinterpreted and developed in the light of new situations. This can be seen even at a single work-place. Factories and offices sprout idiosyncracies, and pass through many stages of change. Language stretches to enable people to speak of their varied work situations in fresh ways.

I can now state what I consider employment attitudes are, if that is not already obvious from the previous paragraph. They consist in people's views of their work experiences and current work situations, expressed in words: no more and no less. The interviews and questionnaires, with which we study employment attitudes, are themselves expressed in words, so it is particularly straightforward to relate this definition of the subject-matter to the way in which information is collected. However, what is said has to be understood: its meaning has to be interpreted. So to dispense with concepts of 'needs', 'need satisfaction' or 'motivation', and to see oneself as dealing directly with spoken views, is not necessarily to replace a deep approach with a shallow one. The meaning of what people say may be both subtle and deep.

Evidently, my choice of definition evades the vexed debate on what is or is not an 'attitude', considered as a special kind of psychological entity. Although I shall continue to use the word as a convenient label, I am choosing to work with the more general and flexible material of 'spoken expressions about experiences of work situations'. This may sound over-general; but psychology is capable of giving a definite orientation to the inquiry, even when it is set out in this form. In psychological terminology, I am redefining 'employment attitudes' as 'verbal behaviour about employment experience'. Psychology contains highly developed ideas about the characteristics of verbal behaviour – far more, in fact, than I shall be able to use in this study. The task then remains of identifying which of the ideas will help to analyse verbal material about a particular subject-area, such as employment.

ELEMENTS OF A PSYCHOLOGICAL THEORY

My most basic psychological assumption is that people *organise* their experiences, and their accounts of those experiences. They do not see their work situations as a collection of disconnected pieces. When one interviews them, they talk in terms of themes and interpretations, not of isolated observations. Their reactions to employment are structured; and this is part of a general ability – or, perhaps more accurately, a necessity – of structuring all aspects of experience. This notion of the organisation of psychological experience has never been better argued than by Bartlett[5], but after many years of neglect, it has been applied fruitfully in many fields by the more recent development of 'cognitive psychology'[6].

However, the problem is to apply this general assumption to the analysis of the replies given in questionnaires and interviews about employment. One has to anticipate the *type* of structure or internal organisation in this material. One needs to be more specific.

One contribution comes from the verbal behaviour theory of Dulany[7], which was derived from, and tested by, an extensive programme of experimental research. He was able to achieve remarkably high levels of successful prediction about the verbal behaviour of people in his experiments, by asking them questions about their interpretations of the situation at certain points. So he concluded that some aspects of verbal behaviour were under the control of other internal thought processes, rather than being wholly a reaction to external events. These internal thought processes should not be regarded as private, mysterious, or inaccessible to observation. They appear to have virtually a one-for-one relationship with the way they are reported in speech; if not, the very high prediction rates in the experiments could not have been achieved.

From this work, one is able to draw an important principle for analysing attitudes. This might be called the principle of verbal dependencies. If one is looking for an explanation of some attitude (i.e. some verbal expression), then one should first of all look for the explanation through other attitudes (i.e. other verbal expressions). This does not mean that what people say has no bearing on the real world, or vice versa. But because the internal links between attitudes are complex, and account for a great deal of the variation in any one attitude that is of particular interest, the first step towards understanding must be to study the attitudinal or verbal dependencies.

Dulany's conclusions have been adopted by Fishbein[8] as part of his detailed investigations of various attitudinal relationships. Part of the flexibility given by the principle of verbal dependencies, is that it facilitates distinctions between different *types* of attitudes. Fishbein's work has particularly emphasised distinctions between beliefs, attitudes-to-objects, attitudes-to-actions, and behavioural intentions. (Other distinctions which he has drawn are less relevant to the analysis of employment attitudes, and are not mentioned for that reason.) It will prove useful if these distinctions are broadly explained.

Beliefs according to his definition are rather specific attitudes or verbal expressions concerning *aspects* of some complex object or activity. If one has enough information about a sufficient range of a person's beliefs, one can infer his *attitude* towards the complex object or activity.

Attitudes-to-objects are, roughly speaking, evaluative statements about those objects. They are based upon a summation of the more fragmentary beliefs.

Attitudes-to-actions are also evaluative statements about actions, and based on the more detailed beliefs. However, Fishbein has argued that attitudes-to-actions are necessarily more complex than attitudes-to-objects.

Behavioural intentions are verbal expressions of what a person is going to do or not to do. If one has enough information about a person's attitudes-to-actions, one can predict his behavioural intentions.

These distinctions, and the predicted relationships between the different types of verbal expressions, have been supported by results from many investigations by Fishbein and his colleagues[9]. Their impact in fields of practical application has not been as wide as one might have anticipated, although consumer research is an exception. Perhaps part of the reason for this lack of application has been the burden of theoretical analysis and argument which the ideas have carried with them. As an applied rather than a basic researcher, I have felt free to take ideas from Dulany and Fishbein in a selective way, without enlisting in the cause of their general theories.

THE STRUCTURE OF EMPLOYMENT ATTITUDES

The ideas from Dulany and Fishbein have to be 'scaled up' to apply them to employment attitudes. They themselves considered rather limited ranges of verbal behaviour, whereas employment attitudes cover a very large part of people's entire life experiences. One is moving from the analysis of attitudes considered singly, or a few at a time, to the analysis of many parallel attitudes organised as a naturally occurring domain of experience.

There is one structural implication of Fishbein's ideas which is of central importance for this scaling-up process. 'Attitudes-to-objects', or evaluative attitudes, are presented as depending upon 'beliefs'; but what do these beliefs depend upon? The answer is that 'attitudes-to-objects' and 'beliefs' are to be considered not absolutely, but relatively to one another. Beliefs are themselves attitudes, but of a simpler kind, and they may in turn by explained by even simpler or more basic beliefs about finer details. This suggests that attitudes and beliefs fall into a *hierarchy* of relatively specific and relatively general levels, and there is no definite limit to the number of these levels. This notion can similarly be extended by considering the chain of linkages between attitudes-to-objects, attitudes-to-actions, behavioural intentions, and so on. Fishbein mentions the notion of attitude hierarchies, but does not fully exploit it.

Let us imagine, then, that employment attitudes are hierarchically structured into various levels. It has already been mentioned that a large, naturally occuring attitude domain of this sort will have many parallel attitudes. Putting together these two points, one can speak of employment attitudes as a *hierarchical multistructure*.

This multistructure might consist simply of a *collection* of separate non-overlapping and essentially independent hierarchical structures, each of which represented the attitude to an object. This would be a rather uninteresting and trivial case. On the other hand, the hierarchical structures might be connected or overlapping at various points. When the multistructure for a naturally occurring attitude domain is cross-connected, I shall speak of an hierarchical system of attitudes, or for short, an *attitude system*. The very notion that we are dealing with a naturally occurring domain (rather than an arbitrary collection of topics) suggests that we shall, in fact, be dealing with attitude systems.

Because the cases which Fishbein considered were fairly simple ones with only a couple of hierarchical levels and a fairly small number of attitude variables, the importance of the hierarchical assumption for large-scale naturally occurring attitude systems has not been appreciated. With increasing *size*, hierarchical systems acquire interesting properties which are unlike those of simpler structures. Where there are only one or two variables exerting a powerful influence, then a change in either one of them will tend to have a relatively large effect. When there are many variables, a change in any one will have relatively little impact on the whole. This difference will be accentuated by hierarchical structure.

The theory of the psychological structure of employment attitudes has, in short, four main points:

(i) Attitudes are characterised by dependency relationships with other attitudes;
(ii) The dependencies are hierarchically organised with an indefinite number of levels;
(iii) The attitudes tend to form a system in which the various substructures are cross-connected;
(iv) The system tends to be large, with numerous attitude variables acting together.

Abstract though this framework of principles is, it provides a quite different set of guidelines for the design and analysis of studies of employment attitudes, by comparison with the 'job satisfaction' type of study which is shaped by theories of human needs or drives. It particularly directs attention towards relations of dependence between various kinds of employment attitudes, and towards dividing the attitudes in terms of their hierarchical level as well as in terms of their content.

A convenient way of defining topics to be investigated, suggested by the theory, is to choose dependent variables which will represent those topics. One can then develop an understanding of the topics by considering the relationships to the dependent variables within the larger attitude structure.

Because of the assumption that employment attitudes form a 'multistructure', it is not necessary to focus the entire analysis on a single dependent variable. Doing so might imply a unitary structure, in which all the relationships at lower levels of the system converged as they moved upwards towards some ultimate reference point. If for instance one had several different variables at the top level in the system, a unitary hypothesis might be that these variables were equivalent in terms of their relationships with variables lower down the structure. In a multistructure, however, the highest level variables may have different relationships within the overall system.

In the remainder of this chapter, I shall discuss two types of dependent or criterion variable which have a prominent place in contemporary research into employment attitudes. The first type concerns the concept of *'satisfaction'* with one's employment. This is a long established and widely used concept, but as our comments on 'job satisfaction' theory have indicated, it tends to be used in a rather specialised sense. I shall suggest that it can be used in a more natural manner. We shall also introduce a second, contrasted class of attitudes, those which relate to *future action* on the part of the individual – intentions are the best-known case. These two kinds of dependent variables, together with their explanatory attitude variables, do not exhaust the scope of employment attitude systems, but provide an adequately varied and extensive part of it for demonstrating this theory.

SATISFACTION

'Satisfaction' is so well established as a technical term that it is easy to forget that it is quite an ordinary, natural word. When one interviews people about their employment, encouraging them to talk with vague questions, one continually hears comments such as 'I'm satisfied', 'I get a lot of job satisfaction', or 'the conditions here are quite satisfactory'. It is not surprising that questions about 'satisfaction' should have become common in studies of employment attitudes. There has been a tendency, as discussed earlier, to assume that the word refers to a psychological state of the individual, related to underlying needs or drives. But it is instructive to consider the actual use of the concept in common speech.

One obvious point is that the notion of satisfaction can be applied to very many aspects of life, both great and small. A man may say 'I am satisfied with my new car', or 'I am satisfied with the way my tomatoes are coming along'. In some cases it seems natural to construct a noun phrase such as 'job satisfaction', and that may give the feeling of something technically defined and respectable, a special psychological entity. But that feeling should be resisted, or else one might be tempted to create a whole range of other psychological entities in parallel, such as 'car satisfaction' or 'tomato satisfaction'. Remembering the smaller types of satisfaction can be a useful safeguard against overstating the meaning or significance of the concept.

A person stating that he was satisfied – whether with his car, his tomato plants, or his employment – should be able to amplify or explain his assertion by pointing out at least a few favourable aspects. The 'should' here has a logical sense: to say that one is satisfied, but that one has no reason to be satisfied, it to depart from the normal meaning of the term. This fits into the account given by Fishbein of attitudes towards objects, and also into the theory of employment attitude systems which I have just described. To say that one is satisfied serves as a broad evaluation or judgement, resting on further evaluations or judgements of a more detailed kind. Satisfaction with one's employment will form part of an attitude system concerning employment, and will be a function of other attitudes at lower levels of the system. Among these may be expressions of satisfaction with particular aspects of employment, such as (say) career prospects, working conditions, or personal relationships at work. Each of these aspects of satisfaction or dissatisfaction will in its turn be justifiable and explicable in terms of further detailed attitudes.

Another consequence of this view is that one is no longer tempted to put satisfaction into a special category on its own. To say 'I am satisfied with this job' is not an expression of a qualitatively different kind from saying 'I am happy working for this company' or 'I like working here', or many other expressions.

The approach I have been suggesting, therefore, represents a substantial demystification of the concept of satisfaction. To emphasise this, I propose to use interchangeably the terms 'expression of satisfaction with *x*', 'satisfaction with *x*', and 'general evaluation of *x*', from now on. This convention makes it clear that satisfaction is simply the probability of a verbal expression for the outcome of a general evaluative judgement; and that this is one of many parallel expressions.

FUTURE ATTITUDES

A particularly important kind of attitude is expressed when someone refers to a *future action* by himself. Statements of intention – 'I am going to vote Liberal', 'I will look for a better job' and so on – are the most familiar attitudes referring to the future. But there are several other types, which are more subtly forward-looking. To focus attention on these as an important group, I have coined a clumsy phrase, 'future-attitudes'. These are extremely useful dependent variables in the analysis of attitude systems.

The significance of statements of *intention* has been recognised, particularly as an intermediate step between attitudes and behaviour. As Ajzen and Fishbein have shown[10], attitudes if properly selected can be good predictors of behavioural intentions, and equally behavioural intentions if carefully defined in relation to behaviour, can be good predictors of the latter.

Statements of *preferences*, or wishes, are less obvious examples of 'future attitudes'. In some instances they may not have a clear reference to the future, for such statements are usually expressed grammatically speaking in a timeless present. Indeed if I say 'I prefer Stilton cheese to Bresse Bleu', this may simply mean that I have tended to buy or eat Stilton when given the opportunity in the past[11]. However, examples with a more definite connection with the future are also easily found. If someone says 'I am tired of going to Jersey for my holidays, I want to go the the Isle of Man next year', this is both a statement of preference, and a predictor of what that person will do if given the opportunity next year. In cases such as these, preferences or wishes can be roughly interpreted as intentions, conditional upon some other circumstances.

Choices too, although taking place in the present, have strong implications for future action. Choosing from a menu is in itself an action, but it also commits the customer to consuming and paying for the dishes chosen. Choices are therefore an instance where the distinction between words and deeds, present and future, becomes nicely blurred.

Attitudes to Employment 23

A general attack on these distinctions was provided by Austin in his theory of 'performative utterances'[12]. Austin pointed out that there were many intermediate stages between saying and doing, and that one could point to cases of saying that operated much like actions in their own right. Taking an oath in a trial, placing a mark on a ballot paper, or saying the words 'I do' in the context of a marriage ceremony, are all actions irreversibly affecting the objective situation. Choices, one might argue, are simply rather weaker instances of this kind of performance utterance, the strength or weakness of the case depending on the context in which the words are used.

This brief discussion has, it is hoped, shown two good reasons for stressing the artificial concept of 'future-attitudes'. In the first place the concept brings together a number of instances which are related to one another in interesting ways. In the second place the range of cases which we have described stretches out from the traditionally defined attitudinal domain towards the traditionally defined behavioural domain, not merely bridging the two but overlapping with both. The task of relating attitudes to behaviour may be greatly clarified by working within this intermediate domain. Having introduced the phrase 'future-attitudes', I shall in fact make sparing use of it. Instead, I shall normally use the more natural terms intention, wish, preference and choice, according to context. Nevertheless it is important to remember that they are connected.

FROM PSYCHOLOGY TO SOCIOLOGY

In what was the long accepted view of employee satisfaction, it was envisaged that there would be a direct relationship between satisfaction and behaviour. The review paper of Brayfield and Crockett[13] documents that tradition. It was supposed that the satisfied employee would conform to the requirements of the organisation better than the dissatisfied employee, by producing more, by having better attendance at work, by staying with the organisation rather than leaving it, by adopting its values rather than those of (say) a militant union, and so on. In this traditional viewpoint it has not generally been considered where intentions to act, preferences, or choices, fit into the picture. One might accommodate them either as an intermediate step between satisfaction and behaviour, or as an outcome of satisfaction in parallel with behaviour.

However the problem encountered by the traditional view has always been that these kinds of behaviour show rather a weak relationship to satisfaction, as concluded by Brayfield and Crockett and by others[14]. This causes less of a problem when one approaches it with the kind of thinking developed by Dulany and Fishbein. Fishbein in particular contrasted the *generality* of most attitudes-to-objects (what I have called general evaluations), with the *specificity* of behavioural intentions. Attitudes-to-objects may have only the broadest guiding function, whereas action is usually decided in relation to a particular set of circumstances. So Fishbein introduces attitudes-to-actions (and other intervening factors) to achieve effective prediction of behavioural intentions. Similarly, if one wishes to use behavioural intentions themselves as predictors of other behaviour, one must be sure that the intentions correspond exactly with the types of behaviour in question.

But the evaluations which people express about their employment may not always be as divorced from their intentions, choices or preferences, as psychology would indicate. Common ground may arise between the two, because some 'objects' in the employment situation may acquire special significance as expressions of, or opportunities for, choice and action. They become significant areas of social interaction, and reinterpreted in these terms of the actors in the situation. The more clearly or intensely are objects of the employment situation seen in this way, the more likely it is that the participants will develop related intentions, goals or plans.

Employment attitudes often refer to objects such as pay, working conditions, promotion prospects, or work relationships. These objects do not necessarily present the same possibilities for action to the individual. Some of them may be regarded as givens of the situation, relatively fixed during the time span which is being considered. Others may be seen as the outcome of other people's actions, for example of management or of unions. A worker in a chemical company may accept that the odours and dust arising from the production process are more or less inevitable, or at least beyond the employer's short-term power to remedy. On the other hand the aloofness of the plant manager, or the rules in force regarding the deduction of pay for starting work late, may be considered by the employee to be within the control of the management. Moreover, the worker may feel that either through individual argument or by collective action he can change the rules about pay deductions, but may not feel that he can alter the aloofness of the plant manager. It may simply not be an item for the agenda. Thus the attitudes to these varying 'objects' have different practical significance.

These examples show how essential it is to understand the social situation of work, if one is to understand the grounds for action. If one understands this background, it may be possible to find relationships between attitudes-to-objects and future-attitudes, even though psychology gives no reason for expecting such relationships. But this means that the methods of sociology have to be used in partnership with those of psychology. The type of psychological analysis which I have described in this chapter provides only an abstract framework: it is left to sociology to supply the more substantial ideas which fit within this. That will be the task of the next two chapers.

3 Pay Attitudes and Pay Satisfaction

The psychological structure of pay attitudes may be derived from the theory of the employment attitude system. It has five main features:

(i) Pay attitudes do not comprise a unitary structure but a multistructure; there is no single criterion which integrates all aspects of pay attitudes.
(ii) Pay attitudes are hierarchically structured.
(iii) The explanation of a given pay attitude generally involves many other pay attitudes; pay attitude systems are multivariable.
(iv) Pay satisfaction is equivalent to a general evaluation of pay.
(v) Pay attitudes are in general unconnected with intentions, preferences and choices, but in specific cases links may arise, through features of the situation.

Can one go any further than this somewhat abstract structural account? Is it possible to describe the kinds of evidence preferred in making assessments of pay? And can one explain the significance of the judgement process? To do so will be to move away from a linguistic and psychological level of analysis, into a sociological account reflecting the current social setting of work and pay.

It will be argued that there is a need for two streams of theoretical development, one for further explanation of pay satisfaction, and one for the topic of pay and conflict. This 'dualistic' approach to pay attitudes is a departure from most current thinking on the subject, and the more radical half of the theory concerns pay and conflict, which will be discussed in Chapter 4. The present chapter presents a relatively traditional theory of pay satisfaction. The contention will be that this approach accounts for a much wider range of evidence than it is currently fashionable to suppose.

PAY SATISFACTION AND ECONOMIC RATIONALITY

The interpretation which I put forward for pay satisfaction is that it is, in intention, an economically rational judgement. But the concept of rationality has served an extraordinary variety of uses in philosophy, psychology, economics and sociology. To use the concept for a particular problem, one needs to identify its relevant facets. In what sense is pay satisfaction rational? And in what sense is it *economically* rational?

For an answer, I have turned to Weber[1]. He did not by any means confine himself to one sense of 'rationality': sometimes, for convenience he accepted one of the prevalent definitions advanced by other scientists, such as the notion of rationality as implying optimisation or maximisation of returns. His original contribution, however, was his definition of rationality as the conscious use of *calculation* of means in order to attain goals or ends, irrespective of the actual outcomes of such calculation.

Calculative rationality was, Weber maintained, a significant empirical fact of modern Western society, one which distinguished it from previous cultures. Even where the latter had the means of calculation, and even where they did in fact apply a calculatively rational method in some fields of activity, this did not become extended generally to all branches of life. Only in capitalist society did the calculative principle manifest itself in the questioning and change of all areas of conduct, and only there was it embodied in the fundamental institutions such as work, property and government. In part this could be attributed to the great development of the means of calculation; Weber particularly emphasised the development of money and monetary institutions, although one might point to other parallel developments such as the standardisation and measurement of goods and services. But Weber emphatically denied[2] that the simple existence of the means of rational calculation led inevitably to its adoption. The comparative studies on which he drew provided contrary examples. The prevalence of calculative rationality was a phenomenon in its own right, a reorientation of social ideas.

In practice, of course, calculative rationality manifests itself to greater and lesser degrees in different spheres of action. But pay would prima facie seem to be an area where calculation would predominate. In Weber's view, as in Marx's[3], the development of free markets for wage labour was a critical factor in the establishment of capitalism. This labour market is an excellent example of the distinction Weber drew between rationally oriented and traditionally oriented societies. It freed employment from dependence on other more general forms of social relationships, such as that of caste, and made it solely dependent on measurable economic exchange. And in industrial societies, it seems obvious enough that pay is the main economic fact for most people: in fact, in industrialised countries generally more than 80 per cent of all income is in the form of pay[4]. So the simplest assumption might be that employees' satisfaction or dissatisfaction with their pay reflected some calculation concerning the market price for their labour.

One obstacle to accepting this assumption is that workers in general have poor access to information about the labour market. It has become a commonplace observation of labour market studies that workers have relatively slight knowledge about the going rates in alternative employment, and engage in a surprisingly limited search for information even when they are (by choice or force of circumstance) seeking a new job[5]. Many employers invest in conducting or purchasing wage and salary surveys – indeed, this has become one of the standard tools of pay administration[6]. But the individual worker usually cannot equip himself with a similar arsenal of information, partly because it is inaccessible, and partly because he lacks the resources.

A further difficulty in obtaining estimates of the true labour market situation arises from the existence of 'internal labour markets'[7] within particular corporations. These are both idiosyncratic and heavily buffered against the direct influence of the outside market – the buffering being provided by some combination of custom, administrative control and union pressure[8]. The existence of internal labour markets reduces workers' incentive to be informed about the wider labour market, and makes it more difficult (for employers as well as workers) to evaluate information from outside.

The other main complication which the employee faces is that he is not generally in a stable situation but one that is characterised by change. His own wage is probably changing from year to year, and so is the average wage for his own occupation and other occupations. The real value of wages will be changing due to variations in the cost of living. His personal circumstances will be changing, owing either to his progress through his life cycle, or to other social forces acting upon him[9]. The economic goals which he seeks to satisfy through his pay may themselves be subjected to continuous and periodic revision due to the changing opportunities and desires stimulated by a consumer-oriented society[10]. All these circumstances of change make the assessment of his pay situation more problematical, aggravating his difficulty in obtaining and handling information on the subject.

If one was thinking of calculation in terms of optimisation, or of a precise analytical solution, then the individual would indeed lack the basis for calculation. Assume however that he merely makes his calculation by the most convenient approximate method within prevailing conditions. Such a view of calculative rationality – consistent with much that Weber said[11] – puts a different complexion on the problem. Although his state of knowledge about the current situation may seem sparse, he has his past experience to draw upon. He may receive in any one period relatively little information, but he may be able to supplement those scraps with more general impressions that he has formed in the past, and the impressions conveyed to him from personal contacts – which will in their turn be condensed from past information streams. In this way, he may develop a knowledge of the relative worth of different jobs in the market, and of the desirability of various types of employment. This knowledge may need to be adjusted only by the occasional glimpse of current change.

The internal labour market of the firm may also have its positive side from the (modified) calculative viewpoint. True, external comparisons become more difficult; but they may also become less necessary. If it is reasonable to suppose that the firm has to keep its general wage level in line with the market, the employee can then concentrate on keeping in touch with what other jobs inside the firm are being paid – with differentials, in short. It is worth stressing that when the internal labour market is strong, interest in differentials does not represent a departure from market-oriented rationality towards some vaguer social comparison process: it is a reasonable form of indirect market calculation. This point will soon be developed.

Changes in the wage rates generally, in prices, in circumstances arising from the individual's stage of life, also provide potentially important means of calculation, when considered jointly with the individual's other accumulated experience. From these he can gauge the improvement or decline in what his pay gets for him, his 'standard of living'. Much the easiest way is by comparing his present standard with what he was brought up to expect, or has more recently achieved. The more he can focus upon this as a means of calculation, the less at a disadvantage he is in terms of information, since he is drawing upon his memory of his own past and recent circumstances.

So individuals can continue to strive for a balanced judgement of their position by using these indirect and partial sources of information. There is still the problem of weighing them and integrating them into an overall judgement. This is a point which would have troubled Weber, who felt there was an important distinction between numerical calculation and other types of judgement.

The existence of the means of numerical calculation is an essential requirement for the development of a general rationally calculative orientation in a society, and to this extent one must agree. But at the level of individual psychological process, it is quite another matter. It is doubtful whether there is any better established generalisation from psychology than that humans are naturally capable of integrating a diversity of information to make intuitive, overall estimates or judgements[12].

The difficulties and complications in the way of perfectly rational calculation therefore directly indicate the nature of 'second-best' rational calculation. If the individual has analytical or numerical methods at his disposal, he could perhaps handle information in a highly selective, elegant manner. Being without such methods, however, he clearly cannot afford to ignore any of the complicating factors in the situation. Rather, he should *make use of them as complementary information sources*, as indirect indicators of his true situation, and integrate them in a balanced way by using his subjective judgement. A person whose judgements *are* influenced by the full range of factors which we have mentioned (and others which may become relevant in particular situations) can be *construed as* rationally calculative in intention. One whose judgements do *not* pay attention to these real complicating factors, who focuses on one or another aspect in an exclusive or arbitrary way, or is stereotyped and incapable of adapting his estimation in the face of new information, would be *construed as* departing from calculative rationality.

Rationality is a social phenomenon, and so I have not approached it in a purely formal psychological way, but by analysing the response of people to their real-life situation. The weight of the argument has rested on two points: the assumption that calculative rationality is a normal characteristic of present society, and the identification of particular obstacles and complications (in the case of pay) which people find ways of overcoming or of turning to their own use.

ECONOMIC AND SOCIAL CRITERIA

The preceding discussion has assumed that it is *economic* rationality of which we have been talking. This assumption has to be justified, for there is nothing irrational about pursuing non-economic goals.

There is in fact a large body of opinion – academic, political and popular – which holds that the meaning of pay is in some sense *social* rather than economic. At the theoretical end of the spectrum, there is dissonance theory[13] and its application in the equity theory of pay[14]; and there is a less formalised set of notions often described as reference group theory[15]. In the context of policy discussions, there are the widely held views that fairness and justice are the central values on which pay rests, and the more pragmatic view that comparisons of pay differentials and relativities are of overriding importance[16]. Another connected strand begins on the academic side, with the hypothesis of working-class *embourgeoisement*, and of status striving as the underlying objective of pay, while it has its counterpart in the popular phrase of 'keeping up with the Joneses'.

This body of opinion constitutes the main opposition to the view that pay satisfaction is economic in character. Unfortunately it is difficult to provide a complete discussion of these linked views, because of the impossibility of reducing them to a single formula. However, they do at least have certain common elements. They share a belief in the importance of processes of comparing oneself with other individuals or groups; and they frequently assume, either explicitly or tacitly, that such comparisons involve social values of a non-economic type. In recognition of these linking characteristics, one might label this cluster of theory and opinion 'social relativism'. It is also possible to abstract or to postulate a series of arguments, part logical and part empirical, which underpin various of the theories and viewpoints within social relativism. Concentrating on these common arguments enables a general critique of social relativism to be sketched. In Chapter 1, I pointed out that the available evidence did not support the idea that differentials and pay comparisons were a major source of conflict. Here, the critique will chiefly be of a logical and linguistic type rather than a review of research evidence.

SEMANTIC PROBLEMS OF 'SOCIAL RELATIVISM'

Before considering the more important arguments, we have to face a semantic problem inherent in contrasting 'social' with 'economic' relations. There is nothing discordant about saying that an economic relation is *also* a social relation. Economic relations only exist within a society; their meaning is a social meaning. This is a tautology, not an empirical observation, and it applies to all aspects of social action, economic or other. Put slightly differently, it is part of the definition of sociology to be concerned with human action solely in terms of its social significance. To say that economic relations are social is to accept a definition of them which makes them a part of legitimate social inquiry. If, however, one wishes to claim that economic relations can be reduced to or distinguished from social relations as a matter of empirical fact, then one is logically required to supply some special limited sense to 'social'. Conversely, when one has supplied a special sense for it – e.g. if one defines it in terms of particular observable non-economic value systems – then one cannot claim that economic relations can be reduced to or substituted by 'social' relations except by means of empirical evidence.

The point can be clarified by an example where 'social' and 'economic' forms of relationships are explicitly and legitimately contrasted. Blau's discussion of social exchange[17] emphasises the distinctness of this concept from economic exchange. Economic exchange especially imposes specific, definable obligations on the parties whereas social exchange implies only a vague and unenforceable tendency to reciprocate. Blau takes as a prominent instance the Kula relationship of the Trobriand islanders, described by Malinowski[18], in which gifts are ceremonially exchanged in order to develop bonds of friendship. Various features of this exchange emphasise their non-economic nature. A gap of months must separate the initial gift and its reciprocation, there is no recourse if the gifts are of unequal value, and the transfer of a gift is accompanied by a ritual display of indifference to it, by both parties. Here we see the possibility of defining a 'social' relationship by characteristics which distinguish it from the economic orientation and can be verified by observation.

LOGICAL ARGUMENTS FOR 'SOCIAL RELATIVISM'

Social relativism in the context of pay satisfaction frequently seems to be proposed as a necessary truth. It is maintained, apparently, that such judgements concerning pay would be logically impossible without social comparisons. An illustration of this view is provided by Robinson[19], who states:

Pay Attitudes and Pay Satisfaction

... differentials and relativities are the only way in which a worker can decide whether he is fairly paid. The concept of fairness when applied to wages is inevitably a concept which requires comparisons. It is not possible to decide whether someone is fairly paid until one knows what other people are paid ... Differentials and relativities lie at the very heart of the concept of equity as applied to wage determination.

Although some of the assertions of this passage may be based on observation, the main emphasis is that the *concepts* being used require the comparisons to be introduced of necessity. This is a logical, not an empirical argument.

Before considering this position, however, one must distinguish three assertions which may be involved in it:

(a) Judgements or evaluations of pay require comparisons with the pay of other workers.
(b) Comparisons with the pay of other workers are necessary where the pay judgements or evaluations involve notions of fairness, justice or equity.
(c) Judgements or evaluations of pay are only meaningful when they incorporate the concepts of fairness, justice or equity.

The first assertion can be rejected by providing counter-examples, some of which have previously been suggested. An individual may evaluate his pay by reference to his own past position or to the range of his previous experience of work and pay. He may judge his pay by criteria developed during the long process of socialisation, by notions of what constitutes a normal or appropriate standard of living, and by general expectations of economic progress. None of these require the use of specific reference group comparisons. It is true, of course, that part of his experiential learning may be the acquisition of knowledge or beliefs about one's own and other social groups. But the notion of wide and diffuse experience leading by a process of abstraction or generalisation to the formation of norms, standards or expectations, is quite different from the idea that experience merely enables the selection of particular reference group comparisons in making current judgements.

Similarly, the assertion that fairness or justice, from their very meaning, imply a social comparison process, can be rejected by pointing out other meanings which they have in the context of pay. The meanings attributed to these terms are indeed extremely varied. They may refer to the law or to contract. Moral or normative notions may be involved, as in the idea of what constitutes a decent living wage, or what may be called exploitation. The notion of fairness might be based on values and ideas concerning payment in a just society. Hyman[20] has provided a critique of notions of fairness in the context of pay, and has suggested that the prevalence of definitions in terms of occupational or job differentials reflects not logic but ideology. He argues that, by treating the conventions of wage bargaining as if they were based on logical definition, one diverts attention from deep issues such as the values inherent in competing views of justice and fairness.

A simpler point may also be raised, which leads into the last of the logical type of assertions of social relativism (assertion 'c' above). When fairness of pay is discussed, it seems to be assumed that 'fairness' means much the same as 'justice' or 'equity'. It can have such a sense. But it can and often does have a different sense, which can readily be seen by taking an example from outside the pay area. When someone says 'I got a fair price for my car' this means no more than that the car fetched the going market rate – no strong notion of justice would be implied. Thus is many cases, 'fair' is a general evaluative term similar to 'average', 'decent', 'reasonable', and indeed 'satisfactory'. The negation of 'fair' in some cases may be 'unfair' or 'unjust', but in others it may be 'poor'. When an individual worker says 'My pay is fair' he may mean much the same as when he says 'I'm satisfied with my pay'. The idea that 'justice' or 'equity' are non-economic in character, and are based on qualitative social values, may be relatively appealing. But it is not legitimate to *assume* that these notions can be associated with everyday comments about the fairness of pay. Thus, each of the assertions that social comparisons are a necessary condition of pay judgements may be rejected by means of counter-examples.

EVIDENCE OF MAJOR STUDIES CONCERNING 'SOCIAL RELATIVISM'

It could still be true that, in practice, pay judgements were made in ways that reflected social relativism. This can only be assessed through empirical evidence. The evidence cannot be sensibly reviewed without distinguishing two empirical propositions concerning social comparisons. The first proposition is that people do make comparisons of their pay with the pay of others, and that these comparisons have some influence on their satisfaction. This is plausible, and fits without difficulty into the calculative view of pay satisfaction. The second proposition is that pay satisfaction is completely or predominantly determined by these social comparisons, or that these comparisons form the underlying meaning of pay satisfaction, to the exclusion of economically rational interpretations. This implies not only that the selected comparisons should be significantly related to pay satisfaction, but that the relationships should be large, so large as to swamp influence from other sources. This proposition is incompatible with the view taken here.

The most substantial evidence comes from the studies of Behrend and her colleagues[21], which have already been referred to in Chapter 1 as casting doubt on the importance attributed to differentials and pay comparisons. It is worth dwelling on some of these findings. The surveys gathered workers' spontaneous comments on what they thought would be fair pay increases, and why. The reasons workers gave certainly included occupational differentials, but this was outweighed by items such as the rising cost of living, the last pay increase received, the current going rate of pay increase, and general discontent among the bulk of manual workers with their low incomes. 'Images' of fair pay, to use Behrend's term, seem much more a matter of personal experience than of any comparison process.

Other studies, not directly concerned with the fairness of pay, nevertheless cast light on the relative strength of economic and social interpretations. Thus, the Luton study by Goldthorpe and his colleagues[22], which concerned in part the *embourgeoisement* hypothesis, found little evidence of striving for higher social status among workers with high pay and high instrumental orientation. Huber and Form's study[23] in an American industrial town similarly provided evidence that need for material goods, not social status, was the prime reason for desiring increased income. Both these studies used supplementary questioning to eliminate the possibility of an interpretation in terms of status or class aspirations.

When one turns to studies frequently cited in support of one or another variant of social relativism, one finds that the results in general do not provide any test of the advocated theories against competing interpretations. This is well illustrated by Patchen's survey[24] of the choice of pay comparisons made among workers in a Canadian oil company. The study focused on pay comparisons as an area of intrinsic interest, and did not concern itself with pay satisfaction in wider terms. The detailed and coherent relationships identified leave little doubt about the reality of pay comparison processes. It would, however, be incorrect to infer that this study casts doubt upon the economic rationality of pay judgements. In the first place, it collected no evidence of the relationship between satisfaction with pay comparisons and satisfaction with pay as a whole. Moreover, the oil men chose their pay comparisons in a manner which can be viewed as economically oriented. For instance, those with better education and better chances of mobility of employment were more likely to select comparisons with people earning more than themselves — which could be a natural reflection of realistic economic objectives.

Similarly, in a recent review of Jaques's[25] theory of equitable payment, Cameron[26] pointed out that results supposed to confirm the theory might equally be explained by simpler factors. Normally, alternative explanations were not tested in the studies reviewed.

The conclusions from research studies are, first, that social-relativistic interpretations have done nothing to displace calculative economic interpretations of pay satisfaction; and second, that the evidence is less conclusive than one might have expected, because few investigators have directly tested the issue.

TESTING INTERPRETATIONS OF PAY SATISFACTION

This lack of direct testing need not persist. In fact, 'social relativism' may be particularly useful in providing a contrasting position to economic rationalism, and so suggesting more explicit testing methods. In many social science investigations, one finds that a theory is tested only against the null hypothesis; with large samples from survey data, such a test tends to be rather weak. The situation could often be improved by finding competing theories and pitting them against each other by means of decisive tests. Here is a case in point.

The first such test has already been suggested in the previous section of this chapter. An interpretation in terms of calculative economic rationality is *wider* than one in terms of social comparisons, because it includes social comparisons among its explanatory material, but permits other types of calculation as well. According to social relativism, pay satisfaction should be *completely* explained by attitudes to pay comparisons. According to the economically rational viewpoint, attitudes to pay comparisons provide only *part* of the explanation of pay satisfaction; attitudes to other aspects of pay will also be significantly involved. So the first test of the two positions concerns the *number and range* of pay attitudes significantly related to pay satisfaction. Within this general test, one may also single out a more specific contrast between the reference group comparisons of social relativism, and pay judgements which are based on personal standards derived from accumulated individual experience. One might call the latter '*self-referent*' sources of pay attitudes, to stress the contrast with the '*group-referent*' comparisons of social relativism. Self-referent comparisons include the type of judgement described by Behrend[27], where the individual compares his standard of living with his experience of past years, or his future rate of pay increase with the trend inferred from previous years. Such comparisons are particularly sensible for the individual in times of rapid change of pay rates, cost of living, or standard of living. A person considering these factors may talk in terms such as 'pay progress', 'advancement', or 'cost of living increases'.

Perhaps one should pause here for a moment to remember *why* self-referent comparisons generally fit into an economically rational viewpoint of pay. Personal experience enables the satisfactoriness of pay to be judged, without recourse to external comparisons, precisely because there is an economic framework of employment and pay, within which the individual's perceptions can accumulate. The existence of monetary measurement frees individuals from social comparison standards.

Another type of self-referent judgement standard is what has often been called the 'effort–reward bargain'[28]. People certainly do make statements about whether their pay is reasonable in relation to the work or responsibilities expected of them. Such a judgement depends, according to my interpretation, on personal experience of work, of the effort involved in various jobs, and the different rewards available by moving to more or less demanding jobs.

To test the theory proposed here against social relativism, therefore, one can consider whether group-referent comparisons dominate in explanations of pay satisfaction, or whether these kinds of self-referent judgements have at least an equal part to play. If it is the latter, then economic rationalism is the theory supported.

But there may still seem to be an escape route for social relativism. Its advocates might argue that the *apparently* self-referent judgements are *covertly* based on group comparisons. In particular, 'equity theory' as expounded by Adams and other social psychologists[29] proposes that satisfaction is based upon a comparison of one's own effort–reward ratio with the perceived effort–reward ratio of a selected comparison person or comparison group. So, in this view, the apparent self-referent notion of an effort–reward judgement is *combined* within a social comparison process.

However, with only a slight shift of emphasis the same test procedure as already proposed can be applied here. For equity theory entails that the effort–reward ratio creates positive pay satisfaction only to the extent that the comparisons on which it is supposedly based are seen to be fair. So, when pay comparisons are held constant in a joint analysis, the effect of the effort–reward ratio on pay satisfaction should disappear. If however one considers that effort–reward judgements have a separate basis from intergroup pay comparisons, their effect on pay satisfaction will be independent and will persist even when the group comparison effects are controlled.

4 Pay Systems, Authority and Conflict

Conflict, as it is normally understood, involves intentionally hostile action. In linking pay attitudes to pay conflict, therefore, one has to show how attitudes can lead to the formation of hostile intentions. In Chapter 2, however, I argued that there was no logical or psychological basis for linking attitudes-to-objects (e.g. to pay) with attitudes-to-future-actions (e.g. intentions) whether hostile or otherwise. The link between the two can only be a substantive one, arising from the social meaning of the situation which underlies both types of attitude. Thus a theory linking pay attitudes to conflict is not a special kind of attitude theory, but a sociological theory of conflictful situations which happen to involve pay.

My discussion of organisational conflict again begins with Weber. It is remarkable that some modern writers, for example Crozier[1], have tended to characterise Weber's descriptions of modern organisations as being exclusively rationalistic. This must be rejected. As Parsons has commented[2], 'never does he (Weber) treat an empirical problem without explicit enquiry into the bearing of power and authority factors on it. Indeed this constitutes one of the few major axes of his whole treatment of social phenomena.' In view of the current neglect of Weber's contribution in this area, it will be worthwhile to review briefly some of the concepts which he developed.

For Weber, authority was an essential feature of all social organisation, and only the basis on which authority rested varied from one type of society to another. In the modern bureaucracy, the basis of authority is of the rational–legal type. The holders of office tend to have been selected on the basis of their technical competence rather than of their social rank or hereditary entitlement. Their authority resides in the office which they occupy rather than in their own personal power, and this bureaucratism is often of a legally prescribed and limited type.

However impersonal is the exercise of authority in the rationally-oriented organisation, it remains essentially authority, and as such it is liable to be resisted and to generate *conflict*. Weber gives several reasons why modern organisations may experience particular tensions and strains which stimulate conflict. For instance, the way in which such organisations force people to occupy strictly limited roles, is one which inevitably generates individual frustration. Emphasising this point by a paradox, Weber sometimes spoke of the irrationality of the rational organisation[3], meaning by this that in order to function rationally as an organisation it often had to suppress or deny the values and interests of its members.

Another source of stress is the tendency for individual holders of office to extend their powers and to appropriate to themselves the powers of their office. So they contradict the legitimacy of their own authority. But this leads to a further point. The legitimacy of authority under a rational–legal regime is perhaps much weaker than under a traditional regime. The emphasis on rationality leads to a general questioning and scepticism about the very basis of authority itself. The definition of the boundaries and limitations of authority may be continually open to renegotiation, depending on what new evidence or new arguments can be advanced. For these and other reasons Weber saw that the type of authority required by the modern organisations was peculiarly weak and unstable in its character, and thereby exposed to the effects of conflict.

Weber's discussion of the basis of authority in modern society, and its weaknesses and problems, has not been superseded. However there are more recent contributions which add and amplify certain aspects. One such contribution is that of Dahrendorf[4], who, as part of a more general analysis of the theory of classes, provided a meticulous logical and conceptual analysis of conflict.

There are two aspects of his argument which are of special importance. First, he points out that it is part of the *logic* of imperatively co-ordinated organisations – that is, organisations characterised by having roles in some of which the incumbents give orders, and in others of which the incumbents obey orders, – that there should be conflict. The potential for conflict must be assumed to exist wherever there is inequality in terms of domination and subjection[5].

Dahrendorf takes pains to emphasise that this is essentially a point of logic, rather than an empirical observation. He does not himself give a direct logical demonstration, but it is easy to provide one. An order may be either obeyed or disobeyed: this is part of the meaning of the word 'order'. Putting it another way, it is meaningless to give an order to a person to do something which he would inevitably do in any case. The purpose of an order, one might say, is to ensure that a person does something which he might not otherwise do. But in as much as orders may be disobeyed, the giving of orders implies a measure of conflict. For conflict, as Weber defined it, is the performance of an action in spite of someone else's will. The existence of conflict, therefore, as Dahrendorf maintains, is entailed as soon as we admit the existence of organisations with bosses and subordinates. The actual extent of the conflict may be great or small, and it may take many forms. These are matters for investigation in particular circumstances.

The second significant part of Dahrendorf's exposition concerns the way in which he deals with an objection to the conflict viewpoint. This objection – which is not only an academic but a popular one – concerns the 'common interest' of ownership, management and workers. According to this viewpoint, the existence of common interests between the different parties in modern organisations should lead to the reduction or complete elimination of conflict. The success of industry leads progressively to prosperity which reaches all members of the working population. As it does so, and the material dissatisfactions and wants of the population are eliminated, conflict becomes pointless.

Dahrendorf's answer is one which Weber himself would surely have given if the question had been posed to him in this form. It is simply that the conflict which arises out of authority relationships is not to do with self-interest but with power. This is not to deny that there can be conflict which relates to matters of self-interest. But even when there are no issues of self-interest involved, even when the individuals concerned have all attained a high level of personal gratification or well-being, the existence of unequal authority relationships still leaves a core of conflict unaffected. Indeed, if it is true that there is an increasing community of rational interest between ownership, management and workers in modern industry, then one may predict that the issues of conflict will progressively become more and more clearly limited to the area of power itself.

At this point – the question of where conflict is to be found – another contribution is available from Crozier[6]. Through his analysis of State bureaucracies, he has arrived at a number of penetrating observations of conflict. I shall confine myself to pointing out two aspects of his observations on conflict which appear to be particularly useful.

First, he pointed out that the bureaucratisation of authority relationships in the modern organisation had a rather *positive* aspect for people of contemporary culture. (He limited his observations in this respect to French culture, but they appear to be equally applicable to other countries of the Western world.) Through rules and procedures, through prescribed roles, personal confrontation is avoided. So long as the relationship remains within its routine confines, it is painless for both sides involved. There is, therefore, a motivational force which tends to cement the bureaucratically prescribed authority relationships.

But although the bureaucratic process enables much of the behaviour in the organisation to be prescribed, routinised, and made predictable, it is never capable of carrying out this task completely. Around the area of rules and procedures, there is always a margin, more or less great, where uncertainty prevails, and where change can and does take place. It is in this margin of uncertainty, argues Crozier, that conflict is concentrated. It is over the matters which are not fixed and prescribed that an individual or group may attempt to gain an advantage over other individuals or groups, to make his own working situation more secure and predictable at the expense of others. In these margins of uncertainty the game of power continues unceasingly, and its purpose is not primarily the material advantage of one side or another – in this Crozier is clearly in agreement with Dahrendorf. Rather it is one of modifying relationships or perhaps more frequently of simply maintaining them unchanged. For Crozier sees power in terms not only of appropriating the position of others, but of securing and guarding one's own position relative to theirs. Conflict may be engaged in to achieve change but also to resist it, and even to reduce the very possibility of change by constricting the margin of uncertainty.

One does not necessarily agree that the area of conflict is always confined to the margin of uncertainty. The circumstances under which conflict may become wider and more threatening to the basic structure of a bureaucracy are matters of great interest. Crozier's account however shows how conflict can persist in this limited sense. One of the difficulties in discussing industrial conflict is that the term has connotations of large-scale and perhaps even violent struggle. It is hard to come to grips with the reality of small-scale everyday conflict, and to understand its workings. The observations and concepts introduced by Crozier scale down the grander general theories of conflict into these everyday terms.

I can now summarise the main points from my review of contemporary theories of industrial conflict. I started with Weber's general viewpoint of authority as an inescapable feature of social organisation. For our own industrial society, I proposed that Weber's account of the rational–legal basis of authority was still the best available description. This account placed stress on the authoritarian nature of modern industrial organisation, and pointed out how the rationalistic orientation of industrial society might tend to create more, not less, tension and conflict around questions of authority. In Dahrendorf's work the logical basis of this argument was clarified, and it was pointed out that conflict was inseparable from an authority relationship. Moreover, the content of conflict was not self-interest, but the relationships of domination and subjection implied by authority. For Crozier, on the other hand, this general societal view of conflict was supplemented by a view of conflict in the microcosm of everyday organisational life. By introducing the notion of marginal uncertainty in power relationships, Crozier provided a method of identifying where conflict is most likely to be focused.

PAY SYSTEMS AND CONFLICT

It is now possible to show how attitudes towards pay can be related to indicators of potential conflict in organisations. The link is supplied by showing in what way pay issues participate in organisational conflict. From the preceding analysis of conflict relations in industry, *pay is predicted to be a focus of conflict in so far as it acts as part of the authority structure of an organisation.* Let us now discuss how this takes place.

Pay enters into authority relations because it is an *administrative system*. While emphasising the role of wages and labour markets in the development of an economically oriented society, Weber also attributed great importance to the role of the administrative system of pay in the development of modern bureaucracy. In contemporary organisations, pay is not simply a sum of money doled out to each recipient on the basis of personal favour, but a complex system in which the relationships between the pay given to various recipients is determined by virtue of rank, service in the organisation, performance of specified tasks, and so on. Pay is typically dispensed by professional administrative staff according to a schedule of rules applied impersonally to all the organisation's employees. Since Weber's time, the elaboration of pay systems has continued and in some large organisations the rules and systems of pay may be found described in manuals running to scores of pages.

When I maintain that the administrative pay system is part of authority, I emphasise that I am referring to authority *systems*, rather than the personal authority of a business owner or a manager. In some cases, systems of authority and individual authority are closely associated, but in modern large organisations the distinction between the two is important. For although managers go about making decisions and giving instructions to subordinates, these expressions of authority direct only a small fraction of the organisation's activities. To a much greater extent, the activities are programmed and controlled by standard systems and procedures operating in an impersonal way. Yet for all their impersonality, these control systems are designed by managers and technical specialists, the main group in which organisational authority is vested, and the systems are an expression of their will.

Pay systems serve to differentiate the lump sum of pay into various parts, and to provide rules governing the dispensation of these parts. In doing so, the pay system resembles other types of control system within the organisation, and like other types of organisational controls, it has a clear and straightforward practical justification. If any area of action in a complex organisation is to be administratively controlled, it is generally necessary to divide it into units of sufficient uniformity and separateness to make possible clear measurement. Rules also must be sufficiently discrete and detailed to be capable of unambiguous application. Division into identifiable components is the essence of control. And the purpose of a control system relating to pay is consistent with the tendency of organisations to secure ever improved effectiveness of operations. If pay is seen as an effort–reward bargain, then the purpose of pay systems may be to ensure that the bargain is bilaterally observed. Even if there is no problem concerning observance of the bargain, there is still the need to make the activities of labour calculable and predictable rather than variable, hence facilitating the large-scale co-ordination of the enterprise.

There is therefore no need to question the rational purpose of the pay system, provided that one also recognises its character as an authority system. The provisions of the pay system, to a greater degree even than most other control systems in organisations, are enforceable. For example, rules relating to reduced payment in sickness, or deductions for late arrival at work, are routinely applied in the calculation of the pay packet. Such rules will in general be written, they will be formally notified to the employees, perhaps embodied in a contract of employment, or in a rule book sanctioned by agreement with a union. Attempts to circumvent rules may lead to the sternest disciplinary measures which the organisation has at its disposal. Falsifying attendance records is as likely to lead to dismissal as arriving drunk at work or striking a supervisor. The pay system represents industrial authority at its steeliest.

In addition to its rational function as a control system, the administrative system of pay is continually used both by management and by employee groups as a lever to develop or maintain power positions. Over and above the economic significance of the pay system both for the organisation and for the employee there is a symbolic significance in the pay system. The condition of the pay system reflects the ascendancy of management or of workers, or the relative importance of various groups of workers. For this reason much effort is invested in the struggle around the pay system, irrespective of the direct economic returns. And for this reason too, the pay system is a particular focus for managerial and worker ideologies.

Thus Behrend[7] pointed out that incentive payment systems for production workers had gained wide support among managers, based on a system of beliefs about properties of these incentive schemes which had not, and could not, be verified; nor had management shown much inclination to seek verification. One might infer that belief in incentive systems served covertly to support the ideology of managerial authority. If workers can be assumed to work effectively only under the continuous pressure or inducement of an incentive system, this bolsters the belief in working class inability to practise self-control or to volunteer effort. This in turn reinforces the need for strong external control, and for managerial authority as an essential requirement for the achievement of economic ends.

A notable feature of conflict around the pay system is that its magnitude bears no general relation to the importance of the aspect involved. Quite minor aspects of pay, even one might say trivial ones, are frequently the source of intense and lasting conflicts. The lengths gone to in order to win a point are quite out of proportion to the apparent importance of that point. For example, Roy[8] describes the sustained campaigns by his fellow machine-shop workers to nullify new rules and procedures instituted by management. If, however, we view pay conflict as part of a wider struggle over authority and power, the observation is no longer puzzling. It is as predicted in Crozier's development of the theory of bureaucratic conflict. These minor issues of pay systems, generally arising out of recent or continual changes, are a point where leverage for power can frequently be exerted by the participants in the struggle.

PAY ATTITUDES AND CONFLICT

This view of pay conflict can be translated in terms of pay attitudes. The basic assumption is that industrial organisation is based on authority, and that authority provides the continuing source of conflict. Payment systems are a part, a signal part, of the authority structure. Opposition to the pay system, or to some aspects of it, is a form of opposition to the authority system in general. Because the pay system enters in a detailed way into the everyday working lives of employees, reactions to it are likely to become an influential part of the individual's conscious thoughts, and to be represented in his attitudes. Attitudes expressing opposition to the pay systems will tend to be associated with other forms of opposition to the authority structure. In as much as the individual is able to take action to express his opposition, and to develop intentions or goals for future action, these too will be expressed in the form of 'future-attitudes' (see Chapter 2). Wherever in a particular situation one is able to identify a ground of conflict, and to show how opposition to the pay system fits into that ground, one is in a position to develop hypotheses linking attitudes to pay with intentions, choices or preferences expressing conflict.

The theory which I am proposing leads to particularly strong predictions. Attitudes to the pay system according to this theory, may or may not be related to pay satisfaction, irrespective of whether they are connected with attitudes towards conflict. The two kinds of relationship arise by different paths. Attitudes to the pay system are capable of being related to conflict even when these attitudes are unrelated to all other aspects of pay satisfaction. And I expect no aspect of pay satisfaction to be related to conflict, once the influence of attitudes to the pay system has been held constant.

The theory also involves predictions about the antecedents of conflict, which reach wider than attitudes to pay systems. Conflict arises from stresses in authority relations, and these stresses can develop in areas other than pay systems. So one expects to find situations where both pay attitudes and non-pay attitudes are related to some common attitudinal measure of conflict. In these cases, the non-pay attitudes like the pay attitudes should be interpreted in terms of authority relations. The process of testing the theory of pay conflict therefore requires that one investigates simultaneously attitudes to pay systems, attitudes to other aspects of pay, general satisfaction with pay, attitudes to nonpay aspects of authority relations, and attitudes expressing conflict (usually intentions, choices or preferences). By looking at the network of relationships among these attitudes, one can obtain multiple tests of the theory. These should result in the demonstration of an attitude structure with two diverging branches. The predictions are summarised schematically in Figure 4.1.

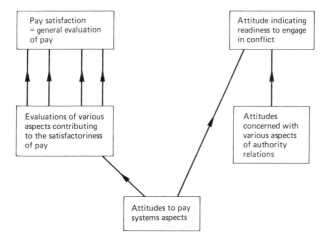

FIG. 4.1   The predicted structure of pay attitudes

5 The Case-Survey Method

The theories presented in the previous chapters have been of two kinds. They have been partly *formal* or *structural* – saying something about the way in which systems of attitudes are organised. And they have been partly *substantive* – making predictions about which aspects of a situation will be more important or less important in explaining various attitudes towards pay and conflict. In the present chapter, I describe a set of methods which enable these theories to be tested in a reasonably systematic and integrated manner. It combines statistical analysis of survey data with qualitative description of particular organisational situations, and I call it the 'case-survey method'.

THE STATUS OF SURVEYS

There is probably rather a wide range of opinion among social scientists about the uses and capabilities of survey methods. The approach adopted here does not accord with much of the conventional wisdom, and so it may be useful to discuss briefly some of the issues at stake.

While surveys are an accepted method of investigating *substantive* issues – usually these investigations are undertaken by sociologists – they are not generally accepted as tools for the study of *formal* or *structural* problems in psychology. Studies like those of Dulany or Fishbein described in Chapter 2, are experimental in nature, and use only a small number of simple, artificial verbal items. The idea is that the fundamental features of psychological structure can appear most clearly when the complexities of attitudes towards real topics have been stripped away. And this approach, the classic experimental method, has a long record of justification by results.

However, accepting that the experimental method is a fruitful one does not entail rejection of survey methods. Each has its appropriate level of application. The approach adopted here has been to use the

The Case-Survey Method

guidance given by experimental findings for redesigning survey methods. If one wishes to use the notions of contemporary cognitive psychology, and apply them to the analysis of complex and naturally occurring cognitive structures, then non-experimental methods will be necessary. In fact, there is a history of discontent among cognitive psychologists with the limitations imposed by classical experimental methods. The most complete critique was provided by Brunswik[1] who developed new experimental designs which in some cases resembled observational surveys[2]. One of Brunswik's central points was the need to understand individual behaviour as a function of the complex natural environment. Subsequently, the need for psychologists to turn to methods of other kinds than laboratory studies has been argued by Barker[3], Campbell[4], Simon[5] and Miller and colleagues[6], among others. Among non-experimental methods, computer modelling has had the greatest development and its successes have been documented in a large literature[7].

But even though many cognitive psychologists may be prepared to agree that experimental methods have limitations, and that other methods should be developed to augment them, they may still be reluctant to accept surveys as an appropriate method for their field of study. Is this not too coarse a tool to capture the fineness of cognitions? Do not the long strings of complex questions required by surveys introduce all manner of uncontrolled variation in responses — varied interpretations, order effects, and so on — which will swamp the relationships of real interest?

Doubts and reservations of this kind are both reasonable and answerable. The answer to them does not lie in counter-arguments, methodological debate, etc., but in practical experience and empirical testing. Whether or not surveys are equal to the task of investigating cognitive structure can be investigated by designing surveys, collecting data, conducting statistical analyses, and either demonstrating or failing to demonstrate the theoretically required relationships.

In adopting this rather pragmatic stance, I am aware that doubts of a more general kind have been expressed about survey methods, by some sociologists as well as by some psychologists[8]. These raise the whole issue of the meaning of the information obtained by surveys. To answer these questions directly would require a long detour into linguistic analysis, and I feel that this book is not the right place for a debate of that kind. The discussion in Chapter 2 should go some way at least towards indicating my position on these issues.

Another area of concern among specialists in survey analysis is the

50   *The Hidden Meaning of Pay Conflict*

process of statistical validation which should properly precede the drawing of conclusions from the results of a survey. In fact, a large programme of developing and applying statistical validation procedures has accompanied the research described here. However, since this programme has been reported in detail elsewhere[9], and since it is likely to be of interest only to survey statisticians, I have decided not to include it in this book.

The remainder of this chapter, accordingly, simply describes the survey procedures which have been developed, without engaging in any more general discussion of methodological issues. It is hoped that these issues will be sufficiently resolved by the actual results to be presented.

OUTLINE OF THE CASE-SURVEY METHOD

The method applies survey techniques within a particular organisation to investigate the situation there. A standard set of measures applicable to any organisation is neither used nor considered something potentially desirable. Rather, independent investigation of each situation leads to the development of a survey questionnaire which brings out the features of special interest. And although the quesionnaire-survey enables the theories to be operationalised and tested, the full interpretation depends equally upon a qualitative account of the situation: a 'case analysis'.

There are a number of stages through which the case-surveys typically pass, even though there may be particular departures from the standard pattern. These stages may be summarised as follows:

(i) The initiation of the survey and the establishment of its terms of reference.
(ii) A preliminary study of the organisation, incorporating collection of documentary evidence, discussions of various types with managers, and interviews and group discussions, of an unstructured or semi-structured nature, with a sample of the organisation's employees.
(iii) A qualitative assessment of the main issues present in the organisation, and the formulation of hypotheses.
(iv) The design of a survey questionnaire, including pre-testing procedures and modification.
(v) The selection and grouping of questionnaire items to repre-

sent the variables of theoretical interest, and the specification of formal tests of hypotheses.
(vi) The collection of survey data from the members of the organisation.
(vii) The application of statistical methods in order to test the hypotheses.
(viii) The interpretation of findings in the light of the earlier, qualitative investigations.

Although most of these stages form part of familiar social survey procedure, the detailed approach is sometimes sufficiently different to require further description.

Preliminary Investigations

Considerable stress was laid on building up a description of the situation in the organisation, by means of a preliminary investigation. Generally there were four sources for this investigation: published documents, internal documents, management discussions, and a sample of unstructured interviews.

Published sources, when available, were mostly of value for understanding the background to the industry and its historical development. An example of this was published studies by the National Economic Development Office on the hotel and catering industry[10]. Internal documents, such as personnel statistics, job descriptions, organisation charts or internal memoranda were mainly of value in establishing the company's policies, both commercial and in the personnel field.

The initial discussions with members of management were useful in a more qualitative way. They tended to provide impressions of the nature of relationships between management and employees, and of tensions in this system of relationships. They revealed recent management actions and policies, and future plans and intentions were also sometimes stated. One was able to develop some view of the history of the organisation, its current state and some of its future choices.

The remaining part of the preliminary investigation occupied a very considerable proportion of the total time required for the survey. It was a series of interviews and group discussions with a substantial sample of the organisation's employees. These interviews and group discussions (groups consisting of usually three employees) were as far as possible unstructured and free-flowing. Occasionally one or two standardised questions were included to focus on particular issues, but, for the most part, the employees were simply asked to describe what it was like to work in the organisation, and to report their likes and dislikes. The purpose of these free discussions, which generally continued for about an hour, was to identify recurring issues or topics, and to get an appreciation of the natural form in which these topics were discussed by the employees.

While much of the material produced in interviews of this kind is fairly stereotyped from one survey to the next, it is also the case that quite a wide range of situation-specific points are generated. Salient issues can readily be identified, using only the simplest content analysis procedures, because of their continued recurrence.

No special sanctity attaches to this mixture of preliminary investigations. In one organisation which will be described later, documentation was very full and the other procedures could be correspondingly shortened. None of the studies to be reported here made use of systematic observation[11] or of ethno-methodological procedures, but these would certainly not be without their value. What needs to be stressed is the importance of a *sufficiently extensive* preliminary investigation, irrespective of what methods it incorporates. The preliminary investigation should be enough to give some view, independent of the survey, of the main forces at work in the organisation, and thus to provide a framework for interpreting the survey results themselves. This is essential for the *substantive* aspects of the investigations.

Questionnaire Design

The questionnaires have been constructed in accordance with conventional principles of social survey design, and it will not be necessary to describe these in full detail.

Probably the most important point is that the questionnaire was composed of a mixture of standard and special-purpose items. The standard items reflect the fact that many features of work experience are common to most organisations – examples are feelings of boredom or interest in one's work, or feelings that promotion prospects are adequate or inadequate. The non-standard or special-purpose items reflect tensions and change processes inside the organisation – and they arise also from the extensive preliminary investigation of each organisation's situation. Examples are questions to do with features of payment systems having a particular importance in a company, or questions probing staff unionisation issues at a time when they are first emerging. Such items as these need to be designed in a way which is sensitive to the local situation and its nuances, and equally the results from such questions require a knowledge of this context before they can be sensibly interpreted.

While I stress the hybrid quality of the questionnaires' make-up, it should not be imagined that their appearance or style was unorthodox. For practical reasons, the questionnaires in the case-surveys to be discussed in this book were all of the 'self-completion' type – that is, answered by the individual from written instructions rather than in a face-to-face interview. Their style was largely governed by this requirement. All items, special-purpose as well as standard, were simple, short and self-explanatory, and could be answered by a forced-choice procedure. Visually, there was no way of distinguishing standard from special-purpose items, especially as all were presented (with a few exceptions) in a randomised order.

Incidentally, no claims are made for the superiority of self-completion questionnaires over personally administered interview schedules. The choice has been made more on the basis of matching survey resources to survey demands, than of any methodological preferences. Recently I have directed several small surveys, examining various aspects of pay attitudes by personal interview methods. Some aspects of the results are referred to briefly in a later chapter. However, the results which I present in detail are drawn solely from the surveys using self-completion questionnaires, since these have been larger and more complex, and therefore permit more comprehensive and rigorous testing of the theories.

The Selection of Questionnaire Items to Represent Theoretical Variables

We can now examine the way in which each survey questionnaire embodied the research issues of particular interest. An important notion of the psychological theory advanced in Chapter 2 was that employment attitudes form a natural domain or area of consciousness. The items in a questionnaire would not necessarily give exhaustive coverage of this domain, but should constitute a reasonably wide sampling of it, if one were to obtain an idea of its structure. The preliminary investigation provides some assurance of this, provided that the full range of topics identified through this investigation have subsequently been incorporated in the questionnaire.

It is the *range* of topics or issues included which is important, rather than the number of items or exhaustiveness of the questionnaire. Since for some purposes there is a great advantage in being able to include all questions in a single analysis procedure, there is also an advantage in keeping the numbers of items reasonably small. As a result of many trial analyses, it has been found that an appropriate selection of about 30–40 questions suffices to represent both the structural features and the substantive hypotheses. How is the selection made from the larger questionnaire, which may contain 100 or more items? It is, essentially, an exercise in judgement based on one's understanding of the content of the items. However, the composition of the selected items may to a limited extent be checked by confirmatory statistical analysis.

To test the theories, questionnaires included items which could be designated as the criterion variables. These served two purposes, depending on the type of analysis in which they were used. For testing the psychological theory of attitude systems, they were high-level variables which could conveniently be used to lever out the structural relationships. For testing the theory of pay attitudes, they were variables attributed a particular substantive meaning or significance, from which other relationships could be predicted. In some instances, the same items served as both structural and substantive criterion variables.

One criterion used solely for purposes of structural analysis is the 'overall satisfaction' item. In this the individual rates his satisfaction as an employee, taking all aspects of his employment into consideration. Many writers have given this item a major substantive interpretation as an index of morale or of motivation[12]. On the other hand, the appropriateness of such an interpretation has often been questioned[13]. It is important to stress, therefore, that these substantive interpretations are completely irrelevant to the use of the item in this research. The only interest of the 'overall satisfaction' item for our purposes is that it is a very general, high-level evaluation of the existing employment situation, and is clearly distinct from other criteria which are also of interest. No particular significance is attached to the notion of 'satisfaction'; questions worded in other ways would be equally appropriate provided that they were equally general high-level evaluations. (For further clarification of this point, see the discussion of the 'satisfaction' concept in Chapter 2.)

A criterion variable which sometimes takes part in a structural analysis, and sometimes in a substantive analysis, is that of 'overall pay satisfaction': that is, an item evaluating pay in the most general terms. Such an item may be used to reveal the way in which pay attitudes have a similar multi-level structure to employment attitudes as a whole. But it is also given a substantive interpretation in the pay theory: such general evaluations are expected to be made in a manner which reflects an economically rational orientation.

The third type of criterion variable relates to future action, usually in the form of an intention, preference or choice. From the point of view of the structural analysis, it is purely this formal or grammatical property of the item which makes it suitable as a criterion variable. In practice, though, the items of this type have been included in the survey design because they have a particular substantive importance, as expressions of organisational conflict. While it is usually easy to decide whether a particular item is or is not a 'future-attitude', it is a more complex matter to define what also makes it an expression of conflict.

The difficulty may be seen in some of the extremely wide notions of conflict that have been used by sociologists in recent years. A limiting case of this tendency is March and Simon's[14] definition: 'conflict occurs when an individual or group experiences a decision problem'. This definition does not even require that there should be more than one party to a conflict. Again, Fox[15] in various discussions of industrial conflict has treated any indication of a difference in interests between employers and employees as an indication of conflict. Thus he proposes labour turnover and absenteeism as signs of conflict, though these have often been used elsewhere as signs of morale.

An individual's actions may conflict with the interests of his organisation, but this may not be the intention or the meaning of the action. He may for instance leave the organisation because he sees an opportunity for personal advancement elsewhere. This action may be detrimental to his present employer, yet no hostility may enter into the situation. On the other hand, the individual may leave because he feels oppressed by an authoritarian style of management, because he feels insecure or powerless in his dealings with the company, and because this is the only means of escape from these stresses. This would be accepted, on my definition, as a genuine example of conflict, because it constitutes a *meaningful response by the individual to pressures arising from authority relationships.*

So the identification of criterion variables which reflect organisational conflict always presupposes an analysis of authority relations in the organisation. As explained in Chapter 3, the area of stress or pressure is often concentrated in a relatively narrow and shifting margin around the authority system. This focal band of conflict is very often defined by recent organisational changes. The constraints on and opportunities for action by the individual also vary from one situation to another. For all these reasons, the design of items to represent conflict is always situationally specific and has to be justified by means of the case analysis.

Hierarchical Division of Items

An essential feature of the theory of attitude systems is the principle of hierarchical ordering of items. In order to submit this principle to test, it is necessary to divide the items into hierarchical levels, and this is a further requirement for survey design. Formally, the problem is to find a method of classifying all the items of the questionnaire according to the hierarchical level. There are two possible approaches to this problem. A panel of judges could be used to sort the questionnaire items by level, and one might then check the agreement between them statistically. The alternative is to use an objective or logical method, establishing a set of rules whereby items can be classified deterministically.

The former approach would be more appropriate if one considered that the classification was essentially dependent on taste, feeling or opinion. In this case variation between judges could be an intrinsic feature of the psychological judgement process. If however the task is considered to be logical or linguistic, so that variation between judges would reflect only their varying degrees of competence, then the deterministic approach is more appropriate. One should only fall back on the judgemental approach if one cannot develop a set of rules under which levels of generality can plausibly be established.

It has in fact proved possible to define a set of deterministic rules. The main feature of the classification procedure is the use of an ordering relation between questionnaire items: 'is an aspect of'. Using it, one finds those questionnaire items which are aspects only of the most general or high-level criterion variable, and not of any other variables. These one calls the 'middle-range' variables. The remaining variables in the quesitonnaire could be sub-divided into further levels in principle, but in practice one generally finds that three levels suffice: the high-level criterion variables, the middle-range variables, and the remainder, which may be called the 'lower-level' variables.

When one turns to attitudes to pay, one can follow a similar approach. The most general pay item would be some kind of broad evaluation of the satisfactoriness of pay as a whole. The remaining pay items have to be divided into those that are relatively broad, representing one of the main aspects considered in the general evaluation of pay, and those that relate to relatively specific details. The latter tend to concern aspects of the administrative pay system, as pointed out in the discussion in Chapter 4. So the hierarchical division of the pay items corresponds roughly to the substantive division between pay levels and their rational evaluation on one hand, and pay systems as a form of administrative control on the other hand. The parallel between the two classifications of the pay items is not necessarily perfect, however, and in some instances there can be an overlap.

Operational Hypotheses

One can now state the types of hypotheses which can be formulated operationally. There are in fact three types of hypotheses, which to some extent interlock with each other. *First*, there are formal or structural hypotheses concerning the attitude system, taken as a whole. *Second*, there are hypotheses concerning attitudes to pay, which are in part formal and structural, but in part substantive. And *third*, there are hypotheses concerning the explanation of conflict in particular situations within organisations; these link up with the substantive hypotheses concerning pay.

When one considers the structural or formal hypotheses, the notion that attitudes have an hierarchical structure is fundamental to the whole approach. Once the variables have been divided up into three or more levels, this may be put into the form of a specific hypothesis. If the variation in the criterion variable is substantially explained by a relatively small number of middle-range variables, and if relatively little additional explanation of the variation is added by introducing a large range of lower-level variables, then one will state that the hierarchy hypothesis has been supported.

Moreover, since the lower-level variables are expected to act on the criterion variables indirectly through the mediation of the middle-range variables, one would expect the middle-range variables *by themselves* to account for variation in the criterion variable to about the same extent as the lower-level variables *on their own*.

A corollary of the hierarchical hypothesis is that we expect that the variation of the criterion variable will be accounted for by a function of many, rather than merely one or two, other attitude variables. If only one or two variables completely dominated the relationships with the given criterion variable, then one would feel that the hierarchical hypothesis was less meaningful.

The third formal hypothesis concerns the view that employment attitudes form a multistructure. This can be tested once at least two distinct criterion variables have been defined at the highest level of the structure. The hypothesis is then that an appropriate function of the variables to explain one of the criterion variables will not be appropriate for explaining the other. Alternatively, given an objective procedure for selecting variables from an initial set to be predictors of each of the two criterion variables, one will obtain a different optimal selection in the two cases. Tests of this type can be achieved using 'overall statisfaction' as one criterion and a suitable 'conflict' variable as the other.

The hypotheses concerning pay in part correspond to the structural or formal ones. One expects to be able to show that overall satisfaction with pay is an hierarchical function of many other pay variables. Also, that different pay variables enter into varying relationships with different criterion variables. However, I also introduce a more substantive content into these hypotheses. I hypothesise, in accordance with the interpretation given to economic rationality, that the variables having the main explanatory power in relation to overall pay satisfaction, will include not only variables concerning comparisons with social reference groups, but also comparisons that are self-referent. It will not be possible to eliminate the self-referent variables by statistically controlling the group-referent variables. I hypothesise, also, that no one or two of these variables will predominate over the others in explaining overall pay satisfaction.

There are, similarly, substantive reasons for expecting attitudes to pay to have various functions within the multistructure. Overall pay satisfaction, and its main explanatory variables of the broader evaluative type, will be related to overall satisfaction. However, attitudes to the administrative pay system will be related to the attitude variables selected to represent organisational conflict – *in as much as* the pay system is itself a focus of organisational conflict. Yet the pay system variables will at most be weakly related to overall pay evaluations; and overall pay evaluations will not be related to conflict.

The subject of conflict itself is treated in essentially a single hypothesis. This hypothesis is that attitude variables concerned with aspects of authority, power and control systems in the organisation will to a significant extent explain the criterion variable representing conflict in the organisation. Those variables which explain the conflict criterion will include attitudes towards the administrative pay system, wherever in the situations which are being considered this forms an area of organisational stress, though elsewhere this would not necessarily be the case.

This description has covered in perhaps tedious detail the build up of the variables and the way in which this leads directly to the formulation of hypotheses. This has, however, provided a basic framework which may help to present the individual case-survey analyses in a reasonably naturalistic manner in later chapters.

Methods of Statistical Analysis

The emphasis placed on treating attitudes as a system demands a systematic approach to statistical analysis. The hypotheses about employment attitudes as a whole require analysis of 30–40 variables simultaneously. But not all the problems and hypotheses are of this magnitude. The hypotheses concerning pay attitudes often involve sets of about half-a-dozen variables at a time. Different techniques have been applied in the two situations, but each technique involves a simultaneous, multivariate analysis.

A basic requirement of the statistical methods is to handle *relationships*. All the hypotheses, without exception, are concerned with the relations between many variables; none is concerned with measures of location or with comparisons between means. Inevitably, one must in practise specify some relatively simple model of relationships, rather than trying to consider all the possibilities.

Because it is assumed that attitudes are hierarchically ordered, in most cases one is dealing with *dependency relationships*. The criterion or reference variable can, in statistical terms, be designated the dependent variable, while other attitudinal items are designated the independent variables. This focusing upon the relations between a set of independent variables, and a single dependent variable, in itself simplifies the analysis.

For the larger analyses, I have made use of multiple regression, one of the most widely used techniques of analysis in the social sciences. There are however technical problems with multiple regression, on which there has been a growing literature in recent years[16]. These have required a number of preliminary analyses to validate the use of the technique. The results of these have proved satisfactory, but for reasons already explained, it has been decided not to present the details here. However, it should be noted that the regression analyses reported in the following chapters have always been carried out using the most cautious and conservative procedures. This means that the strength of the findings will, if anything, tend to be understated.

Wherry[17] has suggested that insufficient sample size is a common cause of spurious multiple regression solutions. Two of the surveys reported in this book could not be faulted in this respect, since they had 669 and 2436 respondents respectively. The third survey however had only 118 respondents, so multiple regression analysis was not used in this case.

Where a small set of variables is being considered, it has proved possible to use the more powerful and flexible technique of multiway contigency table analysis. The most familiar type of analysis for survey data is the simple two-way or three-way cross-tabulation. Multiway contingency analysis takes tables of this type, but ones of larger dimensions, and considers how the individual variables, and relations between the variables, account for the distribution of frequencies in the cells of the table. Several recent reviews of the models and techniques are available[18]. The practical drawback of the technique is that it can manage relatively few variables, even with large sample size. But it provides excellent analyses of tables with up to five or six variables in our two larger surveys. Its use in the third, smaller survey is not practicable.

The multiway table analysis produces parameter estimates which resemble the standardised coefficients of regression analysis, but the interpretation is different in an important way. In regression, the unit of analysis is the individual respondent, while in contingency analysis it is the cell total. So in this latter technique, one is dealing with 'grouped' rather than individual data. In our case, one is considering how far the occurence of various combinations or 'profiles' of attitudes can be explained by a set of simpler relationships among them. This seems a realistic approach for a social science investigation, where purely individual variation generally has little theoretical significance.

The Interpretation of Findings

The use of multivariate analysis in the social sciences is often associated at present with notions of searching exhaustively through data in order to find best-fitting models of the relationships[19]. This, emphatically, is not the approach intended here. In fact, I can see little interest even in the precise numerical estimates of the parameters, proportion of variance accounted for, etc. The approach is one of hypothesis-testing based on strictly *a priori* theoretical analysis. I am interested in making broad inferences or judgements about the underlying theories on the basis of the tests of hypotheses. Alternative models are considered only when this approach helps to overcome technical problems, or leads to a sterner test of the hypothesis of interest.

When hypotheses are being formulated in a particular case-survey, the situation is interpreted in terms of the general theory, and meanings are attached to events and circumstances which appear important. This process of interpretation can also take place in the reverse direction. There may be special features of the findings which are consistent with the main hypotheses yet in some way go beyond them. It may be possible from these to understand the situation more fully, and perhaps to give a fuller meaning to the theory in that particular case. This interplay between theory and findings appears one of the valuable possibilities of case analysis. Evidently, though, this requires once again a qualitative form of interpretation rather than a strict inferential one.

Another aspect of this relates to the question of dynamic interpretation of a cross-sectional study. In a longitudinal study, clearly, the dynamics are part of the design. With the case-survey method, one can to some extent reconstruct the dynamics of organisational change processes from the preliminary investigations and from a general understanding of the industry and the social setting in which the single organisation is placed. But the dynamics of attitudes cannot be reconstructed from single-survey evidence. This lack has to be supplied from the theoretical framework. In order to interpret the attitudinal data fully, one has to utilise the general propositions and ideas derived from the theory. In other words, there are aspects of the theory which can directly be considered and tested within the set of data, but in other respects the theory is used to take us beyond the data.

6 The Hotels

The hotel industry, like some other service industries, is of great antiquity. However, its emergence as one of the major industries of most Western countries probably dates from the period of modern travel, especially business travel, and of the growth of public annual holidays. This has required the development of a large work force, which has been superimposed on a base of traditional working methods and practices[1]. Many of the more expensive hotels and restaurants attempt to maintain the trappings of a past age, which have died out in most fields of life. Hotel and restaurant customers often demand a level of service which reflects this previous tradition and adopt a dominating and punitive style in their relationships with the members of the hotel or restaurant staff. This type of relationship is underlined and perhaps preserved by the custom of 'tipping'[2]. The prevailing style of management in the hotel industry seems to be in tandem with this feature: overtly authoritarian and punitive[3]. Public reprimands of members of staff remain a standard ploy for placating irate customers.

The hotel employee's relationship with his manager is emphasised in a number of ways by structural features of the employment situation in the industry. One such feature is the casualness of much recruitment practice. Many of the subsidiary posts in a hotel are held to require no special experience or skill. Large numbers of staff are employed on a part-time, temporary or seasonal basis. For some posts, foreign staff are engaged through agencies, often on short-term work permits. There is a corps of mobile workers in the industry, alternating between holiday resorts in the summer and cities in the winter for their employment. A further structural feature has been the failure of unions to develop membership in the hotel industry. Faced with small units dispersed over all parts of the country, unstable work forces, and managements who are generally hostile to unionisation, the unions have had little chance of success.

Hotel staff remain among the lowest paid group of occupations in this country. Moreover, relatively few of them have benefits such as are enjoyed by many other working groups, for example pensions, sickness and disability payment schemes, or paid holidays above the statutory minimum. Hours of work are often long or inconvenient, being geared to the needs of customers, who require hotel services mainly in the early morning and evening and less so in normal working hours. There is little standardisation of personnel policies or provisions in the industry, and with few exceptions there is an absence of disciplinary and grievance procedures to protect staff. 'Hire and fire' methods have been typical.

The single personnel problem of the industry which has received most attention has been its remarkably high rate of labour turnover[4]. The factors which have already been described – client–staff and management–staff relationships, structural instability and poor material conditions of work – have all been accorded importance, greater or lesser, in various explanations of the labour turnover phenomenon.

THE HOTEL GROUP

Many of these points applied, with various degrees of force, to the situation observed in a study which concerned the employees in seven hotels forming part of a larger hotel chain. A variety of background information, collected during the case-survey, helps to bring the situation then into focus:

(i) 'Staff booklets' used in several of the hotels visited were examined. These proved to contain detailed instructions to staff concerning points of good manners towards 'guests', clothing, personal hygiene, but no description of staff conditions of employment, facilities or privileges. In short, the booklets emphasised the duties of service but not the rights of employment.
(ii) Although the hotels were part of a large group, the individual hotel managers enjoyed substantial autonomy within financial budgets. It was up to the individual manager to decide how to achieve his revenue budgets, how many staff and of what type to employ, what rates to pay them and what conditions to give them.
(iii) Staff perceptions of managerial authoritarianism formed part

of the survey investigation itself. It was found that staff perceived a predominantly authoritarian style of management, and to a large extent, accepted this as a natural state of affairs.

(iv) The survey questionnaire also included a question relating to 'tipping'. The majority of staff of all types accepted tipping, and hence (it might be inferred) their dependency relationship towards customers.

(v) Staff turnover data were available for each hotel. Only one of the seven hotels had a turnover rate of less than 100 per cent per annum (where turnover rate is defined as: number of terminations divided by average number of employees per time period). The remainder had turnover rates in excess of 150 per cent per annum and in two cases in excess of 200 per cent per annum.

(vi) In one hotel, a more detailed analysis of labour turnover was available over a period of three months, showing the numbers who were dismissed as well as those leaving for other reasons. The proportion of dismissals was 20 per cent of the total.

But though in these respects the hotel group appeared typical, it also had distinctive features. The hotels studied were only a small part of a much larger organisation. As was the case with many of the leading hotel groups, it had expanded rapidly during the 1960s by a combination of acquisition of smaller groups and chains, and by building new hotels to meet increasing demand. The group appointed a number of main board directors who came from manufacturing industry. Sophisticated financial and marketing control, exercised from the centre, became a feature of the group's management. Similarly, new thought began to emerge concerning the industry's traditional approach to hotel management and staffing.

The state of personnel management in each hotel at the time of the survey was still based on traditional relationships, with the minimum of formalisation. Each manager, working only within broad financial limits, determined on his own authority the main features of the individual employee's working life. The absence of written conditions of employment, of rules and procedures prescribing treatment of employees, point to a largely pre-bureaucratic stage of management–staff relationships. However, the organisation had developed centralised financial control and direction, had begun to emphasise qualifications and career structures in the management sphere, and was actively interested in new rationalised styles of hotel building permitting lower staff-to-customer ratios. Labour turnover, and the difficulty of obtaining staff for expansion of the business, were recognised as major potential problems for the future.

THE PAYMENT SYSTEM

The hotel managers' authority in personnel matters was clearly visible in the hotels' payment systems. First, each hotel manager established basic rates of pay in his own hotel. He was at liberty to vary rates of pay as he thought fit, provided that he kept within his overall pay budget. He was also able to give whatever increases he thought fit to employees; but there was no regular process of reviewing wages. Similarly, he might or might not make arrangements to pay staff a premium for overtime, or for working awkward hours or shifts.

The manager enjoyed another area of discretion over pay, as a result of the 'service charge' system which was applied in these (as in most) hotels. A percentage was added to customers' bills to cover service, and this was, notionally, distributed among the staff of the hotel as a kind of incentive bonus system. In practice, though, it was for the manager to decide what proportion of the service charge went to the employees, and how it was allocated. Sometimes they kept the total wage to the employees absolutely fixed, and merely stated in a fairly arbitrary way that a certain proportion of this wage 'came out of' the service charge revenue. In other cases, they allowed the amount paid to staff to vary in some relation to revenue over a period, but this variable element was kept rather small – much smaller than it would have been if the *whole* of the service charge had been disbursed in this way. Finally, most hotel managers ran a 'points system': different individuals or departments in the hotel were tagged with fewer or more points, and their share in the service charge pay-out was proportional to their points. For example, receptionists and chambermaids were often excluded completely by this device.

The service charge system was a relatively recent development in some of these hotels, and was sometimes described by managers as a method of gradually discouraging the demeaning practice of tipping. Although feelings about tipping were ambivalent – some managers continued to regard it as a valuable incentive to good service – it was generally believed that the practice was declining and would continue to do so. If this was the case, then the manager's control over the service charge system became an even more significant aspect of his material authority over his employees.

THE PRELIMINARY INVESTIGATION

At the time of the survey, approximately 1200 staff were employed by the 7 hotels; precision is difficult, due to the rapidity of staff turnover and poor quality of records. There were 215 staff who participated in interviews or discussions, a proportion of about 1 in 6; in addition, 90 managers and supervisors were interviewed, including some managers in the hotel group's head office.

Three major clusters of topics were discernible: the relationships between management and staff in the hotel; pay levels and methods of payment; and the staff's physical working conditions. The last named of these included responses to many specific aspects of the working environment – the staff canteen, staff accommodation, the ventilation of work areas such as the kitchen or the laundry room, rest room facilities, and numerous others. There was, however, no indication that the comments about conditions had any deeper significance from the point of view of the problems which we are considering in this research. Therefore, we will not discuss them in any greater detail. The other two major clusters of issues, however, were highly relevant to our main research theme.

The many comments made about management referred to such matters as the managers' lack of concern for staff, the way in which staff were 'ordered around' by managers, discipline and frequency of 'sackings', favouritism and victimisation. These comments were of particular interest, both because they appeared consistent with much that had been written about the industry, and also because they concerned managerial control and authority in a particularly direct and obvious way.

The employees' comments about their general level of pay were surprisingly favourable. The main tone of the comments appeared to be self-referent, and a fairly modest type of standard seemed to be applied when making an overall evaluation. For example, people tended to say 'it's a decent wage', 'it's a living wage'; and some of the critical comments also used the concept of the living wage as a reference point. A further interpretative point worth mentioning is that in many interviews employees stated that they were very strongly attached to working in the hotel business, and would not feel able to do any other

The Hotels

kind of work. Hotel work was described as being interesting, different, with something new happening every day. This was sometimes explicitly contrasted with the sameness and monotony of working in a factory or an office. Thus the impression formed from the interviews was that for many employees pay was a relatively minor aspect of their orientations, and they viewed it primarily in terms of maintaining a minimum standard of living.

Comments about the payment *system* were largely dominated by the issue of the *service charge*, and were mainly critical. Many employees contrasted the service charge system with another system which they called the 'straight wage', by which they meant a system without any variable incentive payment.

One group of remarks related to the deceitfulness of the system, as seen by employees. It was only really a part of the wage, but it was put forward by management as being something different. A second, and related view, was that the system was simply not understood. Some staff were clearly mystified about the principles on which the service charge was based or calculated; some it appeared were unaware of the use of the points system as a means of calculation. The third type of criticism was that it was unfair as between different groups of staff. This tended to be said particularly by staff who did not receive a share of the service charge, but not exclusively by them.

Another area of criticism concerned overtime, and the lack of any clear rules for rewarding it. This was sometimes closely coupled with general comments about the amount of work or effort required relative to pay given. Although a less frequently mentioned topic than the service charge, all comments about overtime were unfavourable in tone.

A further mainly critical group of comments about payment systems concerned the methods of providing pay increases for progression, or rather the lack of such methods. The criticism generally made was the absence of any mechanism for reviewing salaries and providing increases or increments; similarly, favourable comments tended to occur where a member of staff had received an increment without having to ask his manager for one. In one of the hotels, there was a link between the question of pay increases and comments about the service charge system. In this hotel, the manager was accused of using the service charge points system as a substitute for pay increases. Instead of giving an individual a pay increase he would increase the number of service charge points for that individual. Thus staff spoke of the manager's practice as 'devaluing' the system.

A CRITERION OF CONFLICT

The preliminary investigation pointed to the significance of various aspects of management authority, including discretionary control over payment systems. How was resistance or antagonism to this authority likely to be expressed, and how could this be captured within the design of a survey questionnaire? In this case, for reasons which have already been mentioned, it was natural to turn to the area of labour turnover as an indication of conflict. It is, indeed, difficult to envisage many ways in which the employee in a hotel can express conflict or opposition to authority other than by leaving the organisation. There is no union activity or other form of collective expression. Direct individual opposition in the form of argument or refusal to obey orders would result in dismissal because of the generally autocratic style believed to be appropriate by hotel managers. Leaving the organisation, however, because it is so widely practised and accepted in the industry, is an even more than usually readily available method of expressing opposition.

It must be stressed that withdrawal from the organisation is not *in general* a measure of conflict. Leaving is an extremely weak, one might say a pathetically or comically weak, form of opposition to authority (it is indeed the subject of many jokes in this sense). Only where an employee is in a virtually powerless position must he turn to this course as an expression of his personal freedom from control. In many organisations where employee power is greater, leaving will tend perhaps to be more economically rational in character, and would then be quite inappropriate as a measure of conflict at the individual level. And even in the case of the hotel employees, one must accept that many employees will leave not as an expression of conflict but for other reasons. As usual, when one moves from theoretical concepts to empirical variables, the sharpness of distinctions is blurred and one has to make judgements of degree.

The criterion measures used were, as explained in Chapter 2, attitudes towards future action. There were two questions concerning employees' intentions of staying or leaving. The two versions 'intending to stay' and 'intending to leave' were highly correlated, and it was possible to use either singly as the criterion variable of conflict.

The survey analyses were based on 669 questionnaires, a response rate of about 56 per cent. Although this appears to be a low response, some allowance has to be made for the large numbers of short-stay employees in the hotels, and for a proportion of workers who spoke little or no English. It is estimated that of English-speaking workers with at least 6 months' service in the hotels, about 71 per cent returned questionnaires.

The result will now be presented, in turn, for each of the main hypotheses concerning employment attitudes, pay attitudes and conflict.

(a) *The Psychological Structure of Employment Attitudes*

To test the psychological theory described in Chapter 2, 31 attitude variables were selected from the questionnaire. They covered all the broad standard aspects of employment, together with a number of special points which were shown by the preliminary investigation to be salient in the hotels. These 31 variables were used as the independent or regressor variables in a multiple regression analysis, first using 'overall satisfaction' as the dependent or criterion variable, and then using 'intention to stay' as the dependent variable. All the questions used in the analysis are shown in Table 6.1.

TABLE 6.1. Attitude Items Used in the Analyses (Hotel Survey)

'Middle-range' Attitudes
1. I have confidence in the hotel management.
2. On the whole my present earnings are fair.
3. There is not much variety in my job.
4. I am frequently under too much pressure in my job.
5. The people I work with get on well with one another.
6. I am satisfied with my working conditions.
7. I am happy about the chances I have for promotion.
8. I feel secure about my future with the hotel.
9. I have no confidence in my supervisor.

'Lower-level' Attitudes
10. Earnings in the hotel are good compared with other hotels/other employment in the area.
11. For the work I do my total earnings are poor.
12. Strict discipline is necessary to run the hotel efficiently.
13. The hotel should keep the service charge system, but give staff a straight salary.
14. The different departments do not co-operate as they should.
15. Most people in the company are friendly.
16. Management is not interested in suggestions from staff.
17. My supervisor gives me no credit for good work.
18. I cannot show my abilities in my job.
19. My job is a responsible one.
20. The service charge should be abolished, and staff given a straight salary.

21. I don't believe half the things management says.
22. The service charge system favours some people more than others.
23. I understand the way in which my total earnings are calculated.
24. There is fair payment for overtime.
25. I am satisfied with my progress in earnings since I joined the hotel.
26. My supervisor stands up for his staff.
27. My supervisor is always finding fault.
28. It is unwise to speak your mind in this hotel.
29. I usually hear what is going to happen through my colleagues.
30. I get satisfaction in my job from meeting guests.
31. My supervisor is easy to get on with.

NOTE.

All the above questions are answered: (Definitely Agree, Agree, Disagree, Definitely Disagree).

'Criterion' Attitudes

'Overall Satisfaction'

Taking everything into consideration, how would you describe youself as an employee of XYZ hotel. (Very satisfied, Satisfied, Dissatisfied, Very Dissatisfied?)

'Intention of Leaving'

I expect to leave the hotel within the next six months. (Definitely Agree, Agree, Disagree, Definitely Disagree.)

The variables were also sub-divided into those that were relatively broad or general in their coverage of a particular aspect of employment – the 'middle-range' variables – and those that were at a more detailed level, the 'lower-level' variables. There were 9 of the former and 22 of the latter. Separate analyses were also conducted using *only* the middle-range variables, and then *only* the lower-level variables.

Consider first the regression of overall satisfaction on all 31 attitude variables. The theory I have advanced states that expressions of satisfaction in the employment situation are a function of many variables, and that these variables are arranged in a hierarchical structure, those at higher levels tending to have relatively greater effects on satisfaction than those at lower, more detailed levels. Table 6.2 shows that the regression equation accounts for 32 per cent of the variation in overall satisfaction using binary scoring (this increases to 46 per cent using a continuous scoring assumption), and that 6 of the attitude variables have significant coefficients. Five of these 6 are among the 9 middle-range variables, while only 1 of the 6 is among the 22 lower-level variables. These results are consistent with the hypotheses. Moreover,

The Hotels 71

the variables of which overall satisfaction is chiefly a function are not confined to any one category.

TABLE 6.2. Analysis of Overall Satisfaction

	Rank-Percentile Scoring of all Variables	Binary Scoring of all Variables
Total sum of squares	46.673	144.819
Regression sum of squares	21.166	45.622
Residual sum of squares	25.407	99.197
% variance accounted for by regression	45.6	31.5

Significant regressor variables: Item Label*	Standardised Regression Coefficients
1. Confidence in management	3.18
3. Job variety	2.16
6. Working conditions	3.65
8. Job security	3.20
9. Confidence in supervision	2.90
28. Freedom of speech	2.33

Hotel company $N = 669$; overall satisfaction regressed on 31 variables.
* Numbers refer to the list of items given in Table 6.1.

The full analysis, using all 31 variables, kept the influence of the middle-range variables to its *lower limit* since it treated all the variables at the same level and made no use of the structural assumption of the theory. The regression analysis using *only* the 9 middle-range variables, by contrast, made full use of the structural assumption and therefore provided an *upper limit*. In fact, the 9 middle-range variables by themselves accounted for almost as much variation as the full set of 31 variables, and the coefficients of 8 of the 9 middle-range variables were now significant by conventional standards (see Table 6.3). Taking the two analyses together, one concludes that the hypothesis of the hierarchical structure of employment attitudes is well supported. The main direct effects on overall satisfaction are exerted by the middle-range variables, and one may visualise the lower-level variables acting indirectly through the middle range variables. To convert this picture into a specific quantitative model would require a series of regression analyses to be performed showing the relation of subsets of lower-level variables to particular variables in the middle range level. The analysis of pay attitudes which will follow shortly is an example of one part of such a larger analysis.

TABLE 6.3. Multiple Regression with Overall Satisfaction Using Middle-Range Variables Only (9 Variables)

Total sum of squares	144.819
Regression sum of squares	41.549
Residual sum of squares	103.170
% variance accounted for by regression	28.7

Item Label	Standardised Regression Coefficient
1. Confidence in management	3.92
2. Pay satisfaction	3.22
3. Job variety	2.46
4. Work pressure	2.09
5. Work group	2.02
6. Working conditions	4.69
7. Promotion chances	−1.34
8. Job security	4.33
9. Confidence in supervision	3.63

NOTE.
All variables significant by conventional standards, *except* 'promotion chances'.
Hotel company $N = 669$; binary scoring for all variables.

First however there is another psychological hypothesis to be tested: the notion of the 'multistructure'. The test is obtained by performing an analysis using 'intention to stay' as the dependent variable, and then comparing this with the similar analysis using 'overall satisfaction' as the dependent variable. It will be seen from Table 6.4 that the 31 attitude variables account for about the same proportion of variation of intention to stay as they did for overall satisfaction. Also, the number of variables with significant coefficients was similar in the two cases: 6 in the case of overall satisfaction, 7 in the case of intention to stay. However only 2 variables were common to both sets. And whereas in the case of overall satisfaction the significant variables were concentrated among the middle range, in the case of intention to stay 4 of the 7 significant variables came from the lower-level subset. The 2 dependent variables were therefore predicted by 2 different but overlapping sets of attitudes. Together they comprise a 'multistructure'.

TABLE 6.4. Multiple Regression With Variables Representing Intentions of Staying in the Organisation

	31 Variables Regressed with	
	Overall Satisfaction	Intention to Stay
Total sum of squares	144.819	130.170
Regression sum of squares	45.622	38.970
Residual sum of squares	99.197	91.200
% of variance accounted for by regression	31.5	29.9

Significant regressor variables:

Item Label	Standardised Regression Coefficient
4. Work pressure	2.01
8. Job security	5.46
13. Service charge/straight salary	2.15
14. Work group co-operation	2.48
21. Confidence in management	3.31
23. Understanding of pay calculations	2.67
25. Pay progress	3.15

Hotel company $N = 669$; binary scoring for all variables.

(b) *Attitudes to Pay*

According to the theory, pay attitudes have the same multivariable, hierarchical structure as do employment attitudes in general. The matrix of simple correlations of the pay variables, shown in Table 6.5, supported this forcibly. Clearly, the most general item in this set was the one relating to 'fair pay' in general terms, and this variable had large correlations with the three others that were apart from itself the most general in their reference: 'pay compared with outside', 'pay for work done', and 'pay progress'. These were also highly correlated with each other, though slightly less highly correlated than with 'fair pay'. The more specific, detailed items – 'overtime pay', 'fairness of service charge', and 'pay understanding' – all had very much smaller correlations with 'fair pay', but had in addition some moderate correlations with the three more general pay aspects.

TABLE 6.5. Attitudes to Pay: Simple Correlations

Label*	2	10	11	25	24	22	23
2. 'Pay satisfaction'	1.0						
10. Pay compared with outside	0.5366	1.0					
11. Pay for work done	0.5083	0.3763	1.0				
25. Pay progress	0.5602	0.4534	0.4693	1.0			
24. Overtime pay	0.3085	0.2765	0.2995	0.3373	1.0		
22. Fairness of service charge	0.2297	0.2498	0.3050	0.2101	0.2116	1.0	
23. Pay understanding	0.1618	0.2025	0.1827	0.2920	0.3382	0.1240	1.0

Hotel company $N = 669$; binary scoring.
* Numbers refer to the list of items in Table 6.1.

That the three main pay variables already mentioned provide an adequate explanation of opinions concerning 'fair pay', was shown more exactly by means of a multiway table analysis. In this 'fair pay' was taken as the dependent variable, and in addition to the three pay attitudes a fourth, relating to 'work pressure' was also included because it had a high correlation with the 'pay for work' variable. The three pay variables give an excellent fit to the table. The variable 'work pressure' in spite of its influence on 'pay for work' had no appreciable influence on 'fair pay'.

The next step is to provide an interpretation of these three variables and their influence on feelings about fair pay. The hypothesis is that when an individual makes an evaluation of this type concerning his pay as a whole, he takes account of all relevant factors in a balanced manner: this is 'calculative rationality'. The contrary hypothesis, coming from 'social relativism', is that comparisons with the pay of other groups will have the dominant effect on pay satisfaction. The results show that the satisfactoriness of external pay comparisons was indeed a powerful predictor of feelings about fair pay. Equally powerful, however, were the effects of feelings about 'pay for work' and 'pay progress'. The multiway table analysis also eliminates the possibility that all these variables interact in their effects in such a way that they have to be interpreted as a single entity. The results therefore

The Hotels

are consistent with 'calculative rationality' but not with 'social relativism'.

(c) *Pay and Conflict*

It was mentioned when discussing the results of the interview analysis that rather low standards seemed to be applied by the hotel workers, giving the impression that pay, or at least high wages, were not a particularly important aspect of their outlook on the employment situation. The results of the regression analysis of overall satisfaction confirmed this impression. 'Pay satisfaction' is certainly not one of the large influences on overall satisfaction, and on a conservative interpretation it would not even be considered significant.

Because of this low orientation towards pay in its economic sense, it is all the more striking to find three pay variables of a more detailed kind occuring as appreciable influences on intention to stay, the measure of organisational conflict (Table 6.4 above). Of these three variables, none is significantly related to 'overall satisfaction' and two have very weak relationships with 'pay satisfaction'. Like employment attitudes, pay attitudes form a multistructure. But do the pay attitudes which are related to conflict fit an interpretaion in terms of authority, as the theory requires?

Background knowledge of the hotel industry, and the preliminary investigation in these hotels, suggested that the authority of the hotel manager, and the way employees reacted to that, was likely to be extremely important. The results depicted in Table 6.4 show that there is a very strong effect from 'confidence in management' and 'job security' on 'intention to stay'. This is right in line with expectations, especially as these two attitudes are themselves strongly related and justify a joint interpretation. The manager's relations with staff, and the feelings of security or insecurity resulting from this relationship, can readily be interpreted in terms of his autocratic powers. Similarly, all three pay attitudes which are significantly related to 'intention to stay' can be interpreted as reactions to the manager's discretionary control over payment systems.

'Pay progression', as the preliminary interviews indicated, took on a special meaning for some employees. They thought of the arbitrary and *ad hoc* manner in which the hotel manager granted pay rises. The desire to abolish the service charge system was particularly prominent in the interviews, and it was widely criticised because of the way the manager could manipulate its terms. The third pay attitude having a bearing on leaving intentions – difficulty of understanding pay – was also very probably connected with the arbitrary and ambiguous way in which the payment systems were administered, and this also attracted critical comment in the preliminary interviews.

There was however a partial shortcoming in the analyses. It will probably have been noticed that 'pay progression', as well as influencing 'intention to stay', was strongly related to 'pay satisfaction'. There is no direct inconsistency in these results, but it means that from the point of view of the theory, 'pay progression' has to be interpreted as a dual or composite variable. It partly reflects the stresses of managerial discretion over pay increases, but also it has its usual more general sense, concerning the movement of pay levels for all reasons. It would have been better to demonstrate these two meanings by including additional questions, but this was not provided for in the questionnaire design.

Fortunately, in spite of this shortcoming, the general pattern of relationships from the analyses remains sufficient to support the hypothesis. Pay attitudes divide into two groups, and the existence and significance of the second of these groups – interpreted in terms of authority relationships – would have been hard to predict by means of any other available theory.

DISCUSSION

W. H. Whyte, one of the exponents of the human relations school of social psychology, found in the hotel industry one of the finest examples to support this viewpoint[5]. The study presented in this chapter supports the view that relationships with management are the central feature in the psychological world of the hotel employee. But it also suggests limitations on the human relations viewpoint. First, the hotel employee seeks a wider range of satisfactions, and weighs their importance more evenly, than the human relations school would have credited. Moreover, the analysis has shown the crucial importance of the structural concepts of authority and power in developing an understanding of management–staff relationships in the hotel industry. For the individual employee, relationships with management *may* be in part a matter of obtaining reassurance, sympathy, support and approval, and of being provided with a place in a harmonious social group. But it appears also to be largely a matter of finding a relationship which protects and secures him from arbitrary action or from the threat of the manager's power. Further, this power of the individual hotel manager seems to arise largely from characteristics of the industry, rather than from the personality of the hotel managers. This group of hotels had its fair share of warm, sympathetic, supportive managers, as well as those who were more blatantly autocratic in their methods. Yet the relationships demonstrated were essentially homogeneous across the hotels.

The hotel industry, as already noted, has only recently emerged from a condition in which the individual employee was as much dependent, or perhaps more so, upon the customer or 'guest' as he was upon the manager. To a hotel organisation seeking to develop more rationally efficient methods of operation, the particular relationship between employee and customer must be seen partially as a threat as well as a resource. Indeed as Miller and Rice[6] have suggested, the ambiguous relationships between management, staff and customers are a particular feature of service industry in general as rationalisation advances within it.

An employee in a hotel who can obtain the main part of his remuneration, and his personal satisfaction, from the hotel guest may not be willing to co-operate in the development of more rational methods of hotel administration. His interests as he sees them may lie purely in maintaining his existing relationship with the customer. But as the rational–bureaucratic mode of organisation advances, so does it undermine personal relationships of all kinds, including for example the tipping relationship in hotels. This has provided hotel management with the opportunity to enlarge its area of control and to change the balance of dependency. The pay system provides one means of doing so.

Within two years of this survey's completion, however, the hotel group had designed and implemented a fully standardised national scheme of pay and conditions for all employees. The details of this scheme do not concern us here. It is enough to note that a very large part of the flexibility and control exercised by local hotel managers over the administration of pay was swept away by this change. Authority over pay was transferred from the periphery to the centre.

Can one predict the changes in employees' attitudes which would tend to occur following the centralisation of authority over pay and pay systems? This would depend on the particular form in which that authority was exercised, and the areas of uncertainty in power relationships which it created for employees. The immediate effect would probably be to remove or reduce the effect of the pay system on local conflict, and this might be the more so since, on general grounds, one would anticipate a decline in the power of the local manager due to progressive business rationalisation. But in the long run, the pay system would remain a prime example of the organisation's authority and the individual employee's powerlessness in this industry. The impersonality and remoteness with which that authority would now be exercised would themselves create new forms of anxiety, and a search for new expressions of opposition to authority.

7 The Finance Company

This case-survey arose from the growth of white-collar unionism in the early 1970s. It took place in a financial services company where the National Union of Bank Employees (NUBE) was pressing for recognition. The survey was partially responsible for resolving this situation and bringing the company to grant recognition. It also provided an opportunity to study employees' attitudes as close as possible to the moment when they decided whether to support unionisation.

The financial services company was an excellent example of the continuing progress of bureaucratic forms of organisation. Its main business consisted in providing various forms of commercial and consumer credit, and its profits arose from its ability to earn interest from these loan activities and to collect the repayments in an efficient manner.

The modern financial organisation has succeeded in replacing the somewhat offensive lending and borrowing relationship with a clinical, routinised and professional service. The dispensation of credit to individuals is not a matter of estimating personal worth, but of the application of fixed rules and procedures to impersonal information. Indeed, for the large credit organisation, the elimination of personal judgement and whim in making credit-worthiness decisions is a prerequisite of providing the kind of painless service which the customer requires.

This finance organisation, a particularly large one of its type, possessed these characteristics to a high degree. It had consisted for many years of three main groups. In the front line were the branch offices. These were small, and comprised a few representatives with some supporting clerical staff. The representatives 'sold' the financial service to local businesses dealing with consumers, such as car dealers, electrical retailers, and so on. Second in line behind these, stood a central clerical and administrative service agency. This agency controlled both the flow of money and of information, and ensured that the routine operation was working efficiently. But although a controlling agency, it was still essentially a routine function. The direction of the organisation, the formulation of policy, and the overall design of the systems was vested in the third level, which was also a central function. This third level comprised the directors of the company and their professional expert staffs.

One might have expected that an organisation designed as an efficient credit-processing and cash-collecting machine would have treated its staff in an equally formal and impersonal manner. But until recently it had maintained a type of relationship with its staff which was typical of an earlier period. Business had been built up in the years following the Second World War by a single man who had retained ownership in his own hands, and was described by managers who had worked with him as a typical entrepreneur. In his approach to staff, however, he was described as benevolent and paternalistic. He had avoided any semblance of a formalised personnel policy or system, but his practices were protective and indulgent.

Dismissals apparently were extremely rare, and redundancies unknown in this regime. Loyalty was highly valued, and rewarded by a salary system geared to service rather than to individual achievement. Loyalty had also been a major qualification for promotion to managerial posts, and in many cases posts appear to have been specially created for their incumbents where no promotion opportunities would otherwise have existed. Staff with domestic or personal problems could expect the sympathetic help of the company on an individual, *ex gratia* basis. The overall picture, therefore, is of a style of personal relationship common in an older type of clerical service organisation. This had survived alongside the development of a modern bureaucracy.

CHANGES IN STAFF POLICY

The situation had begun to change when the rule of the entrepreneur had ended less than ten years previously. The company had become publicly quoted, and its board of directors had been reconstituted bringing in a number of specialists from other fields. The injection of outside capital had enabled the company to grow rapidly, and this process was accelerated by the acquisition of other businesses. Both the organisation's central staffs – the clerical-routine and the professional-specialist – were greatly expanded as a result.

As part of this wider process, a completely new centralised personnel function was created for the company, about four years before this study, and a far-reaching review of personnel policy commenced. The two senior personnel managers brought in to head this development both came from manufacturing rather than service industry. They were professional specialists in the personnel field, and viewed the task of personnel management as ensuring that employees were being properly utilised as an important resource of the business.

Within three years they had planned and conducted a series of measures to change the personnel structures of the company. The requirements of various jobs in the company were analysed, and the jobs were evaluated and graded in relation to one another. The suitability of individuals for filling various posts within the organisation was reconsidered, and in the ensuing reorganisation, some were moved to jobs having greater responsibility, others were moved to less demanding jobs, and some were made redundant. Formalised training was increased, partly to improve the work standards of existing staff, and partly to ensure a supply of sufficiently capable new recruits. On top of this, a staff appraisal scheme[1] was introduced for all employees.

The review of jobs, the introduction of formal training, and the development of the appraisal scheme, jointly pointed towards an increasing rationalisation of the individual's work prospects. A similar rationalisation was also carried out of the company's salary structures and systems. Minimum and maximum salaries were established for each job grade. Increments given for service were abolished as such, and replaced by a system of annual reviews which now had two components.

First, the structure of salaries as a whole was kept in line with the going rates in the external labour market. The second element of the salary review was an individual one, and was based on the performance grading given to individuals by their superiors. To take a hypothetical example, a person given the highest performance grading might be given an increase of 10 per cent on salary, while a person given an intermediate or average grading might receive 5 per cent and a person given the lowest performance grading might receive nothing. This system – referred to as the 'merit review', and officially unconnected with the appraisal system which has already been mentioned – meant that the individual's progression up the salary bracket in which his job grade placed him depended on performance, not on tenure.

THE UNION RECOGNITION CASE

It was after most of these changes had been introduced and made operational that the first developments of white-collar unionism took place in the company. The National Union of Bank Employees began to recruit for members at the main central office where the clerical routines were conducted. A similar smaller office, handling some separate aspects of the company's business, was also canvassed at about the same time. Management took no steps either to encourage or repress the union activity, but a review of the situation was undertaken by the central personnel department.

At this stage NUBE made a formal claim for recognition based on its membership at the main central clerical office. The company rejected this claim, and the union initiated proceedings in the National Industrial Relations Court. However, after recourse to the arbitration procedure of the Industrial Relations Act, the company and the union agreed to use the results of the survey as means for jointly assessing the situation.

PRELIMINARY INVESTIGATION AND SURVEY DESIGN

The survey was, therefore, conducted against time pressure. The free ranging interviews used in other surveys were replaced in this case by a more limited form of investigation in which pre-testing and interview were combined. Following a documentary study of the situation in the company (and fortunately, the various changes taking place were well documented), a draft questionnaire was used as the basis for a structured interview with a random sample of 66 employees which served to 'pre-test' the questionnaire itself.

In addition to the pre-testing/interview procedure, interviews with 40 managers holding a variety of key positions in the organisation were conducted. These were also of a type that was rather different from the normal opinion-centred interview. Their main purpose was to obtain descriptive material about the history and background of the organisation, and the actual events occurring over recent years. It is from this material, together with the documentary sources, that the general account of the company's background which has been given in the introduction to this chapter, has been derived.

The questionnaire in its final form, following modification as a result of the pre-testing/interview procedure, can be divided into four types of items for our purposes. First, there are the commonly used or standard types of attitude items relating to broad, and more or less universal, aspects of the employment situation. Their presence needs no further explanation. Second, there was a fairly substantial list of items which had been generated from the documentary study of changes in personnel policy that had taken place in recent years. The items sought the employees' attitudes to these changes. Changes relating to payment systems were in this case particularly prominent. Third, there was the standard measure of 'overall satisfaction' with the employment situation, to be used as one of the criterion variables. And fourth, there was a set of items concerning unionisation, which could be divided into two types: (a) questions obtaining general opinions about the consequences or characteristics of unionisation, and (b) questions asking employees to state a preference or cast a vote in regard to the unionisation of their own company. The latter were used as a criterion of conflict in the organisation. To explain this will need a short digression before turning to the results of the survey.

THE MEANING OF WHITE-COLLAR UNIONISATION

The growth of white-collar unions is often spoken of as a recent phenomenon. It has in reality an extremely long history. As Lockwood[2] has pointed out, the white-collar union movement was already established on a large scale by the early 1920s and many of its distinctive features had been determined by that stage. By searching back into the history of the period before white-collar unions had been developed, Lockwood was able to build up a graphic picture of the nature of clerical work in the pre-bureaucratic or minimally bureaucratic organisation of the nineteenth century. At this time the number of people in clerical occupations was still relatively small. The individual clerk's organisational position tended to be quite close to that of the owner or entrepreneurial manager. Relatively large decisions and a large scope of authority might be delegated to the clerk. Methods of doing business had not become standardised, so that each organisation preserved its own idiosyncrasies. Moreover, commercial and technical knowledge had not to any large degree been written down or formalised, but resided largely in the persons of the individuals who had the requisite experience.

Thus the clerk possessed, as Lockwood concluded, a considerable degree of *power* in his relationships with the owner or manager. The personal nature of his knowledge could make him virtually indispensable. And, in parallel with this, if not as a direct result of this, the relationships between clerk and owner tended to be personal and individual, rather than standardised and formal: a type of relationship which has come to be known as 'particularistic'. Such a relationship recognised that the clerk had personal claims on the owner, rather than any claims resulting from his tenure of office.

In the modern large commercial or governmental organisation, this pattern of relationships has been swept away. Large organisations tend to require large staffs, routinisation of business procedures, and the documentation and recording of essential knowledge. These changes mean not only a reduction in the economic value of the clerical worker to his employer, but also a weakening in his personal power relationship. At the same time, the concentration of large numbers of similar white-collar workers within particular organisations gave unions the opportunity to organise them. As Bain[3] has pointed out, concentration of occupations is the main structural factor enabling the growth of unions.

The recent history of the finance company appeared to follow the lines of Lockwood's argument, but the processes of change had been delayed and, at the end, accelerated. It appeared natural to me to connect these changes both to the onset of unionisation in the company, and with my theory of pay and conflict. The formalisation of personnel policy, especially payment systems, would create stresses in authority relations between employees and the company. The greater the hostility to the changes, the more likely were staff to turn towards unionism as a means of strengthening or securing their position. So support for unionisation could be regarded as a reaction to shifts in authority relations, and hence an expression of conflict.

Such an interpretation is quite different from the popular or 'common-sense' views about the growth of white-collar unionism. These views connect unionisation with the relative pay levels of white-collar workers, their declining career opportunities, or other material disadvantages. These views could in the terms I have used in this book, be called rationalistic. To be more rigorously formulated and tested, they require a more definite theoretical basis.

A rationalistic approach, which provides a contrast to the position I have taken, is provided by certain parts of the organisation theory of March and Simon[4]. March and Simon did not directly discuss the question of unionisation, but they provided a theory of rationality within organisation, in which conflict was described in largely rationalistic terms. From this theory a number of propositions could be derived about unionism as a form of rational conflict.

March and Simon differ from other theorists in assuming that the whole of organisational conflict can be explained in terms of multilateral deficiencies of rationality itself. The resulting definition of conflict is not only rationalistic but also extremely broad: 'conflict occurs when an individual or group experiences a decision problem'. Under this definition, dissatisfaction with pay, for instance, could be described as a form of conflict.

For a theory of unionism, March and Simon's concepts of attention-focusing mechanisms and group identification are relevant, as well as their definition of conflict. When the individual employee experiences conflict (in the sense just described), he will initiate a search to find some way round the problem. The greater the number of individual goals which are obstructed, the more extensive will be the process of search and, other things being equal, the greater the likelihood of unionisation being focused upon as a solution. This rationalist theory, therefore, rather than focusing on particular sources of unionisation, seems to predict that it is the sum of employees' dissatisfactions with the employment situation which will dispose them towards unionism.

THE QUESTIONNAIRE SURVEY

The data from the questionnaire survey was collected in the early part of 1972. A census design was used, and every facility was provided by the company to enable the resulting large mass of data to be collected economically. All the questionnaires were completed in working hours and on company premises according to schedules agreed by the management. The National Union of Bank Employees also gave the survey its support. It issued letters to its members encouraging them to participate in the survey and to ask others in their own parts of the company to participate. In the event, 2436 usable questionnaires were returned, a 94 per cent response.

It may help to set the scene to present some of the main descriptive findings. First, the survey established that there was a substantial degree of latent support for unionism in the company. While NUBE had claimed no more than an 8 per cent membership, the survey showed that 31 per cent of employees – and as many as 45 per cent in certain places – expressed a direct wish for union representation. Almost

50 per cent of employees stated that they would join a union if one had been recognised by the company. A third of employees, however, stated that they would continue to oppose unionism even if a union had been recognised. These results were sufficient to convince the company of the need to recognise NUBE, and within a short period an agreement between the company and union had been finalised.

At the same time, the descriptive results of the survey seemed to indicate rather strongly that morale or satisfaction was at a high level in the company. Thus 86 per cent of respondents declared themselves either satisfied or better in overall terms as employees of the firm, and a high proportion also gave favourable replies concerning pay, working conditions, job interest, job security, and other major aspects of employment. If, therefore, a relationship was to be found between attitudes to the employment situation and the development of unionism in this company, it was probably not going to be of a crude and simple type, such as a general or widespread disaffection or demoralisation of the white-collar work force. The obvious inapplicability of such naive explanations provides one justification for the more complex type of analysis which follows.

TESTS OF HYPOTHESES

(a) *The Psychological Structure of Attitudes*

The 'overall satisfaction' self-rating was taken as the criterion variable in a regression analysis with 36 explanatory variables. These were classified by the standard procedure into 'middle-range' and 'lower-level' variables, with 9 of the former and 27 of the latter. The psychological hypotheses, it will be recalled, are that overall satisfaction is a function of many variables, and that these explanatory attitudes are hierarchically structured.

The results, which are shown in Table 7.1, generally support these hypotheses. First, the degree of explanation achieved by the independent variables is certainly satisfactory for this type of data, and with a population of such a large size. Forty per cent of variation is accounted for with binary scoring of the independent variables, and this rises to 46 per cent if a continuous scoring method is used. Of the 9 middle-range variables, 7 had significant regression co-efficients. Eight of the 27 lower-level variables were also significantly related to overall satisfaction. So no less than 15 variables in total entered into

The Finance Company 87

the explanation of overall employment satisfaction. Moreover, they cover a very wide range of aspects of the employment situation.

TABLE 7.1(a). Multiple Regression Analysis of 'Overall Satisfaction'

	Binary Scoring of the 36 Independent Variables
Total sum of squares	166.724
Regression sum of squares	67.569
Residual sum of squares	99.155
%variance accounted for by regression	40.5

Finance company $N = 2436$; overall satisfaction regressed on 36 variables.

TABLE 7.1(b). Items Used in Multiple Regression Analysis

Middle-range
1.* I am not satisfied with my working conditions.
2.* The company has a good reputation with outside people.
3.* I like the work I do.
4.* I am happy about the chances I have for promotion.
5.* On the whole my present salary is fair.
6.* The company expects more work from its staff than most companies.
7.* I feel secure about my future with the company.
8. My boss is friendly.
9.* It is unwise to speak your mind in this company.

Lower-level
10.* The company provides good fringe benefits for staff.
11. For people at my level, the chances of promotion are poor.
12. My salary is poor compared with what other firms pay.
13.* The company does a lot to provide comfort at work.
14. The company does not look after its staff.
15. The way the company handles changes make me feel insecure.
16.* I am often bored with my job.
17. I have had good training for the job I do.
18.* There is not enough reward for extra responsibility.
19. The way people are selected for promotion is unfair.
20. I believe that my salary is fair compared with other staff in the company.
21. The appraisal interview has helped me to improve my work.
22.* Salary increases have kept up with the cost of living.
23. The training of new staff is poor.
24. Holiday entitlement should depend on job grade.

25. My job grading gives me too little scope to improve my salary.
26. I have little chance of getting more training in the future.
27.* I am satisfied with the hours that I work.
28. I have not been given enough chance to express my views in the appraisal interview.
29.* I am satisfied with my progress in earnings since I joined the company.
30. My boss does little to develop my skills and abilities.
31. Overtime payment is satisfactory.
32.* From your own point of view, how would you rate your last appraisal interview? (Very helpful/satisfactory/little help/did more harm than good)
33. Everyone doing the same job should get the same salary increase.
34. I have been told the salary range for my job grade.
35. My boss often asks staff what they think before making a decision which affects them.
36. My boss keeps closely in touch with the views of staff.

* Items having significant regression coefficients.

Although the middle-range variables are not so dominant as in the hotels survey, they provide quite a satisfactory account of overall satisfaction. This is shown by a separate regression analysis using only these 9 variables. The proportion of variance accounted for was then 32 per cent – compared with 40 per cent using all 36 variables together. This is shown in Table 7.2.

The remaining psychological hypothesis is that employment attitudes form a 'multistructure' rather than a unitary structure. To test this, 'unionisation preference' was introduced as a second criterion variable. However, in this case a regression analysis was technically inappropriate. Inspection of the simple correlations of employment attitudes with each of the three 'unionisation preference' items showed that these correlations all had the expected sign, but were uniformly of small magnitude, nearly all being between -0.10 and -0.20. The results of a regression analysis would have been unreliable.

Nevertheless, this result supported the view that employment attitudes do *not* form a unitary structure, since the attitudes which were strongly related to 'overall satisfaction' did not emerge here. On the other hand, one would have expected *some* of the attitudes to be more prominent in their relations with 'unionisation preference'. An alternative approach to finding such relations will shortly be described.

(b) *Attitudes to Pay*

It has already been mentioned that the topic of pay had a particularly prominent part in the survey design. In all there were 12 main pay

The Finance Company

TABLE 7.2. Pay Attitudes. Multiple Regression Analysis

Total sum of squares	210.43
Regression sum of squares	102.01
Residual sum of squares	108.42
% variance accounted for by regression	48

	Standardised Regression Coefficient		Standardised Regression Coefficient
External pay comparison	18.10	Overtime pay	−0.17
Internal pay comparison	11.00	Information job grades	−2.72
Pay progress	14.28	Grading and pay progression	1.37
Fringe benefits	2.70	Standard rises (not merit)	−3.02
Reward for responsibility	2.33	Salary information	−0.01
Cost of living increases	4.23		

Finance company $N = 2346$.
Dependent variable 'pay satisfaction', 11 independent variables; binary scoring of all variables.

variables in the questionnaire, covering both attitudes towards broad aspects of pay and attitudes towards administrative pay systems. These could be sub-divided *a priori* into four sub-groups. *First*, there was as usual a single item representing overall satisfaction with pay. *Second*, there were three items concerning major factors in pay: comparisons with external pay levels, comparisons with other staff in the organisation, and satisfaction with one's pay progress in the company. The *third* group consisted of four more specific or concrete aspects of remuneration, namely; the cost of living component in pay, differentials for levels of responsibility, overtime pay and fringe benefits. The first two of these were expected to be particularly relevant to the 'pay progression' item in the previous group. The *fourth* and final group consisted of four items concerning aspects of pay systems. Three made specific reference to grading, which was the basis of the entire salary structure, while the fourth approached (in a somewhat indirect way) the extent to which staff accepted the principle of merit in salary increases.

First, an overall view of the pay attitude structure was obtained by taking the most general pay satisfaction item as the dependent variable and the remainder as independent variables in a multiple regression analysis. The results of this analysis are presented in Table 7.2. About 48 per cent of the variation in overall pay satisfaction was accounted for, and exactly the three variables which were hypothesised to have the most direct effects were the ones having substantial coefficients in the solution. The remaining coefficients were relatively speaking very much smaller. This is consistent with the idea that pay attitudes have a hierarchical structure.

If they do have a hierarchical structure, it is appropriate to carry out a secondary analysis in which the more specific or low-level pay attitudes are used to predict overall pay satisfaction. The coefficients derived from such analysis are to be interpreted as reflecting the total effects of the lower-level variables on overall pay satisfaction, that is, both their direct effects and the indirect effects through the mediation of the three more general pay attitudes.

There were eight of these more specific pay attitudes, but it was possible to reduce this number to five, by eliminating three of the pay system variables by a preliminary analysis. The five specific pay variables selected, therefore, were: fringe benefits, reward for responsibility, cost of living component in salary progression, job grading as it affects the salary ceiling within a job, and overtime pay.

A multiway table analysis was conducted using these as the independent variables and overall pay satisfaction as the dependent variable. It will be seen from the results shown in Table 7.3, that all the specific pay variables had significant effects, as conventionally judged, on pay satisfaction. Moreover, the fit of the model is very satisfactory. Of interest are the particularly large coefficients of two of the five variables: 'reward for responsibility' and 'cost of living increases'. It would be reasonable to call these two variables key factors in pay satisfaction.

The hypothesis that 'pay satisfaction' is a judgement based on a calculatively rational process, rather than one that is dominated by reference group comparisons, is strongly supported by this evidence. This is shown not only by the presence of both self-referent and reference group variables as powerful influences on overall pay satisfaction, but also by the significant relationships of a wide range

The Finance Company

TABLE 7.3. Effects of 'Specific' Pay Variables on 'Pay Satisfaction'

Summary Table of Effects	Standardised Main Effect
Fringe benefits	3.87
Reward for responsibility	7.81
Cost of living increases	9.35
Grading and pay progression	4.14
Overtime pay	2.59

Finance company $N = 2346$.
'Pay satisfaction' as dependent variable with 5 'specific' or lower-level pay attitudes as predictors. Maximum likelihood logit model; X^2 goodness-of-fit statistics: before fitting main effects, 384.82 on 31 df; after fitting main effects, 27.88 on 26 df.

of lower level pay attitudes on overall pay satisfaction. Both 'reward for responsibility' and 'cost of living increases' are most easily interpreted as self-referent attitudes.

One further piece of evidence, already reported but not stressed, strongly confirms this interpretation. In the multiple regression analysis of the entire attitude set on overall satisfaction, shown earlier in Table 7.1, both satisfaction with external pay comparisons and satisfaction with internal pay comparisons have near zero coefficients. But overall pay satisfaction, satisfaction with pay progression, satisfaction with cost of living increases, and satisfaction with reward for responsibility, all have substantial relationships with overall satisfaction.

(c) *The Explanation of White-collar Unionism*

Before describing further analysis of attitudes to unionisation, let us briefly re-state the theoretical argument. Lockwood's theory of white-collar unionism explains why the bureaucratisation of clerical work leads towards the adoption of unions. In the finance company recent years had seen a considerable extension of the bureaucratic method within the field of personnel policy and staff relationships. It was natural to hypothesise that attitudes towards the change in personnel policies would be associated with attitudes towards unionism. In Crozier's terms, one might say that the imposition of the formalised personnel policies created a new margin of uncertainty for employees who were subject to them, in that they became subject to rules which they could neither control nor influence in operation. The establishment of union representation, by creating a centre of power which was capable both of controlling the application of rules and if necessary changing rules, might provide employees with a means of regulating and diminishing this margin of uncertainty.

However, we have already seen that the correlations of employment attitudes with unionisation preferences were slight, and because the coefficients were so small, regression analysis would not provide a reliable basis for selecting variables to develop an explanation of unionisation preference. This does not necessarily mean, however, that the expected relationships between changes in personnel policy and preferences for unionisation do not exist. It shows only that the expected relationships, if they exist, are not strong enough to manifest themselves in individual items. It might however still be possible to obtain the expected relationships by making appropriate *a priori* selection of items in order to form *composite* variables representing the theoretical relationships.

Four composite variables were constructed to explain support for unionism. The items chosen to form them are shown in Table 7.4.

TABLE 7.4. Items Used to Form Composites for Analysis of Unionisation Preference

1. *Unionisation preference*
   I would like to see staff represented by a union.

2. *Formalisation of personnel policy*
   The company expects more work from its staff than most companies.
   More information about job grades should be given to all the staff.
   Holiday entitlement should depend on job grade.
   There is not enough reward for extra responsibility.
   My job grading gives me too little scope to improve my salary.
   Everyone doing the same job should get the same salary increase.
   From your own point of view, how would you rate your last appraisal interview?

3. *Impersonality of managerial relationships*
   My boss does little to develop my skills and abilities.
   My boss is friendly and willing to talk.
   My boss often asks staff what they think before making a decision which affects them.
   My boss keeps closely in touch with the views of staff.

4. *Self-interest*
   The company has a good reputation with outside people.
   I am not satisfied with my working conditions.
   I am often bored with my job.
   I am happy about the chances I have for promotion.
   On the whole, my present salary is fair.
   I feel secure about my future with the company.
   The company provides good fringe benefits for staff.

5. *Attitudes to unions*
   Union membership is a good way of safeguarding jobs.
   Individuals would be better protected against unfair treatment if they were union members.
   A union would get more for staff than staff would get on their own.

NOTE.
For each item, a response that was interpreted as being favourable (i.e. a favourable view or positive employment attitude, a favourable view of unionisation, etc.) was scored 1, otherwise 0. Each composite was then formed as the simple unweighted sum of the responses to the relevant items, and each individual was scored 1 or 0 on the composite depending on whether his score was above or below the median for the survey.

The composite variable of greatest theoretical interest has been labelled 'formalisation of personnel policies'. Because the process of formalisation affects authority relations, it is expected to create opportunities for conflict which may find their expression in unionism. The items chosen to represent the concept were those which referred to specific recently introduced policies. They had been tested in the preliminary investigation to ensure that they were seen in these terms by the employees themselves. The seven items focus on various aspects of job grading, the appraisal system and the merit element in salary. All these, as we have already shown, are directly linked to the underlying rationalising philosophy of change in the personnel management system.

The second composite variable concerned the impersonality of relationships between employees and their managers. Impersonality is attributed a separate role in both the Lockwood theory, and also in other discussions of bureaucracy such as that of Crozier or of Gouldner[5].

The third composite, labelled 'self-interest', represents the competing view of unionisation derived from March and Simon's rationalistic theory of conflict and identification. This has already been discussed, and as indicated the natural way to represent this position is by a composite variable made up of a set of the middle-range variables.

The last of the composite variables is labelled 'attitudes to unions'. By this is meant general evaluations of various aspects of unionism, rather than an expression of personal choice or commitment. It seems essential from a common-sense viewpoint to include some representation of general attitudes to unions in attempting to develop an account of unionisation choice. It is implausible to imagine that unionisation choice occurs purely as a function of what is going on inside the organisation and how individuals are reacting to that. One must suppose that an individual's views of the desirability or otherwise of union representation will depend upon what he perceives to be taking place in society generally. By including attitudes to unions among the predictor variables, one not only improves the fit of the explanation, but one also maintains a realistic assessment of the contributions of the theoretically derived attitude variables within a total picture.

The main analysis consisted of a five-way contingency table, in which unionisation preference was taken as the dependent variable, and the four composite variables were taken as independent. The main result of this analysis is summarised in Table 7.5. One sees from this

TABLE 7.5 Analysis of Unionisation Preference

Chi-Square Goodness-of-Fit Statistics	
Before fitting main effects:	1000.09 on 15 *df*
After fitting main effects:	4.66 on 11 *df*

Summary Table of Main Effects	
Composite Label	Standardised Effect
Formalisation of personnel policy	3.24
Impersonality of managerial relations	0.10
Self-interest	0.41
Attitudes to unions	25.44

Finance company $N = 2436$.
A multiway contingency table analysis, with 'unionisation preference' as the dependent variable, and 4 composite variables (as defined in Table 7.4) as predictors. Maximum likelihood logit model.

The Finance Company

table that the dominant effect is due to the 'union attitudes' variable. However, the variable 'formalisation of personnel policy' also has a substantial and significant direct effect. Neither 'managerial impersonality' nor 'rational self-interest' has an effect of any appreciable magnitude. The fit of the main effects model is excellent, indicating that there are no interactions present between the four composite variables in their effects on unionisation preference.

It is now possible to assess, in a more qualitative way, the outcome of this process of conceptualisation and analysis. The result of putting two theories into a kind of contest with each other seems to have resulted in a fairly clear victory for the theoretical position which has been advocated here. Nevertheless there are some limitations in the results which need careful consideration.

The failure of 'managerial impersonality' to have an effect on unionisation preference is such a limitation. However, the way in which the finance organisation had evolved suggests that this feature of the results is not a serious embarrassment. It seems likely that the nature of the relationships had been impersonal for many years previously. The indulgency and paternalism towards staff was not a result of dispensations by individual managers but rather a norm which pervaded the organisation and originated in the outlook of the organisation's former owner and chief executive. The individual manager's impact on the way in which his subordinates appraise their work situation appears to be relatively small in this organisation.

A second difficulty in the results is the very large relationship between the attitudes to unions and unionisation preference. Undoubtedly these attitudes to unions would have substantial relationships with a variety of other variables not included in the analysis, such as perceptions of the external employment situation or the activities of unions elsewhere. Ideally, one would wish to pursue the analysis of attitudes to unions in much greater detail in order to clarify their nature. In the absence of this, and in the absence of a strong theory of attitudes to unions, there is clearly room for criticism in this quarter.

Nevertheless, although one can always envisage further sophistications of survey design, it is also necessary to make a reasonable judgement on the basis of existing evidence. Although one would like to have a deeper theoretical basis for attitudes to unionism, the empirical relationships obtained with this variable have been both strong and consistent, and the explanation of the entire data structure is clearer when the union attitude variables are included than when they are excluded.

The conclusions on the available evidence, therefore, are as follows:

(a) factors outside the organisational situation have a major influence on unionisation attitudes, and hence on unionisation preference;
(b) of the factors within the organisation, the most powerful direct influence on unionisation preference is employees' reactions to the development of formalised personnel policies, which can be interpreted within a framework of the theory of bureaucratic authority;
(c) employees' more general satisfactions and dissatisfactions, which can be interpreted in terms of a theory of subjective rational self-interest, have no direct influence on unionisation preference.

CONCLUDING COMMENTS

The results have exposed the deficiencies both of attempting to account for unionism in terms of the self-interest of individuals or groups, and of the argument that the role of unionisation is diminished or eliminated by the 'common interests' of employers and employees. The results are consistent with the notion that there are two distinct attitude structures, one related to satisfaction and the other to conflict.

The explanation I have proposed has been that unionism grows out of conflict around authority. But whether such an explanation is accepted as satisfactory, will depend not only on the detailed evidence presented, but on whether it seems to provide a sufficiently realistic and illuminating account of the situation. Here one may experience two obstacles to acceptance. One may feel that insufficient grounds have been presented to make plausible these employees' 'conversion' to unionism. And one may feel uncomfortable about the use of the notion of conflict in such an outwardly contented setting.

Partly, these feelings may arise from the strong emotional tone of the word conflict, as normally used – almost a tabu word in everyday speech. One must remind oneself that conflict can be limited, it can be impersonal in nature, and it can be defensive rather than aggressive. There is no reason to suppose that those employees in the finance company who supported unionisation sought direct confrontation or the overthrow of managerial authority. Rather, they saw, in the changes taking place in the company's policies, elements of uncertainty or potential threat to their own position, and sought about them for some means of re-securing it. A modest enough programme of action, perhaps, but questions of authority and power lie at its centre.

Did the employees, then, correctly perceive the threat to their own position, or did they exaggerate its import? The more formal approach to personnel policy introduced by the company, with its orientation towards task and performance rather than loyalty and indulgence, might, one imagines, be of direct benefit to the majority of employees. But it is not the direct effects of a change in the workings of the authority structure which constitutes the basis of conflict, but the new margin of unpredictability which that creates within power relationships. And rational principles applied to personnel administration, whatever the immediate practical form they take, have longer-term implications of uncertainty. For if staff are to be managed in a rationally efficient manner, then they become a resource to be adapted to changing business conditions and technologies.

8 The Manufacturing Plant

The third case-survey concerns production workers engaged in semi-skilled manual factory work, the workers being represented by a single union. It also concerns an emerging situation of major conflict, in which (within months of the survey's completion) a prolonged strike took place. It is set within an organisation which was at the very extreme in applying rational economic ideas to its operations. All these features make the situation relatively easy to describe and to understand. Much of the research into job satisfaction, payment systems and industrial relations has been conducted in industrial organisations like this one. The main subject of the investigation also has a familiar look to it: it is the incentive payment scheme and the workers' views of this scheme.

The study took place in a single moderate-sized manufacturing plant, but this was part of a very large multinational corporation, with an outstanding commercial record. The plant was under the immediate control of a general manager, but was also part of an extensive centralised management system. Each plant worked to targets and objectives (in the familiar terms of output, plant utilisation, scrap rate, etc.) which were centrally fixed. These targets, and the progress towards achieving them, were conspicuously displayed on a notice board in the plant. A substantial production planning department at the plant received information about sales plans and required delivery of orders and passed information back to a central computer department. Pay and industrial relations, though handled on a local basis, were actually controlled by central specialist staff who were 'on call' to the plants, and could therefore ensure an integrated policy. Finance, capital investment, and budgetary planning and control, were likewise central functions though involving collaboration on the part of plant management.

A further feature of the management system of the company was its high degree of professionalisation. Its main source of plant management was by way of recruiting young graduates in engineering or natural sciences, who went into technical or specialist posts such as quality control, production engineering, methods study, process development, and so on. From these posts, promotion could be gained to line (production) management as well as staff (technical or specialist) management. Promotion often involved moving to another plant, and as the posts concerned became higher in the management structure, it became more probable that the move might be overseas. It was said that once a man was on the management ladder he could expect to move about every three years.

The existence of this highly qualified, mobile pool of managers naturally would strengthen central control, and perhaps justify it. It fitted in with the pursuit of high technical standards, and with the maintenance of universal company policies and operating procedures, which the trained manager would carry with him, and which he would also expect to find around him supporting him in any new post which he assumed.

PERSONNEL POLICIES

The company's philosophy of employee relations was highly developed and was based on a mixture of rational standardisation and line management responsibility, which greatly reduced the need for a specialist personnel function. Many examples of standardisation can be provided. A formalised system of job evaluation and grading, enshrined in a considerable manual, was used for creating the job structure at each plant. It was general policy to establish orderly plant-level union relationships by drawing up at an early stage a full agreement covering in detail the various terms and conditions of employment, and procedures for reviewing them from time to time. Wage rates were negotiated locally, and the intention was to be competitive with rates paid in that area.

As another deliberate and publicly stated principle, the company aimed for a stable work force, and in return provided a good level of security of employment. At the time of the survey the proportion of employees with less than one year's service at the plant was 16 per cent. In the survey itself, three-quarters of the respondents stated they felt secure about their future with the company. The company's continuous commercial success, enabling high rates of growth and relatively few business setbacks, enabled it to provide continuity of employment. Short-time working, lay-offs and redundancies were unknown.

Considerable emphasis was placed by the company on the recruitment of good quality first line supervisors. Whereas the main work force of the plant was locally recruited, and belonged to the neighbouring community, supervisors were recruited much further afield and their selection process was taken very seriously. The proportion of supervisors was high: about one to every seven workers. Moreover, as the supervisor could draw on a very considerable amount of specialist technical support for the production operation — from well-staffed quality-control, maintenance, technical service and industrial engineering departments — he was able to maintain close contact with the hour to hour work of his section.

THE NATURE OF PRODUCTION WORK

The plant consisted of a main machining shop, which cut and finished products from sheet material, in a fairly typical batch production mode. There was also another smaller department, which coated and treated the sheet material by a continuous chemical process, prior to the cutting and finishing operations. For convenience's sake I shall call the latter the coating section, and the former the finishing section.

The type of work organisation required in the two main sections was radically different. Workers on the coating section were jointly responsible for operating a large, single, integrated process plant. They had to work flexibly and co-operatively as a team. In the finishing section, however, each worker tended to have his own machine, carrying out a limited number of operations in the preparation of the finished product. Moreover, while nearly all the workers of the coating section were paid on the incentive system, the finishing section had a much larger proportion of workers paid on time rates only — these were workers either involved in materials handling and transport, or housekeeping activities, or machine work that was too variable to be timed for incentive payment. Even so, the majority of the finishing department workers were on incentive payments.

THE INCENTIVE PAYMENT SCHEME

The incentive payment scheme itself differed as between the coating and finishing sections, but in both cases comprised a mixture of individual and group elements. The basis of the scheme, as normal with incentive schemes, was the establishment of a standard throughput rate for various types of product passing through particular operations on particular machines. A bonus could be earned by producing at above the standard rate. The actual amount of additional bonus earned, relative to some given level of production above the standard rate, was calculated by means of a scale which was built into the agreement on wages with the union. The scale differed from one grade of operator to another – the higher grade operators, who performed more skilful or more responsible work, were able to earn a higher level of bonus. This individual component of incentive applied across the entire range of operator jobs.

The basic difference between the coating and finishing sections, however, was that in the former case the measure of output was based on that of the entire crew of workers, for each batch of product which they processed, whereas in the case of the finishing section, the measurement related to the batch of product machined by an individual worker. In both cases, in addition, correction factors to the bonus calculations were computed. The main correction factors were related to machine utilisation, materials wastage, and scrap rate. These were essentially group production factors, and in many instances the way in which the factors were calculated cut across the performance of any one given group, and applied to the effectiveness of a series of different production groups. It is not surprising therefore that, in the course of the preliminary investigations, it was found that the majority of workers not only in the coating section but also in the finishing section spoke of the incentive scheme as essentially a group scheme rather than an individual one.

The principles of the incentive scheme, the type of formulae used to arrive at bonus calculations, and the procedures used to keep the scheme up to date, had been developed over many years of experience by the company and were applied in a standardised fashion to its operations all over the world. The company's undoubted faith in the scheme was reflected by the amount of effort which they were prepared to invest in maintaining and running it. A team of 8 qualified industrial engineers, headed by their own manager, agreed work methods, timed jobs, and established standards, for a group of only 126 incentive workers. This rather large team of industrial engineers was required because as well as establishing standards initially, all regular production jobs were retimed and re-evaluated about once every 6 months. In addition, a group of 4 clerical assistants was required to calculate the incentive results for wage payment purposes. So, for every 10 incentive workers, there was one technical or administrative person concerned with the incentive scheme. It should also be noted that the industrial engineers were a highly qualified and prestigious group within the plant. Former members of the section had been promoted to management in recent years, and the general level of morale in the section was at an exceptionally high level.

THE PRELIMINARY INVESTIGATION

The survey, which took place late in 1971, was intended as a wide-ranging review of the personnel policies at the plant, of employees' job satisfaction, and of relationships between employees and supervisors or management. No one area was focused upon in advance as being of special importance. The intention was to generate some findings which would stimulate discussion and communication among different parts of the plant, and act as a stimulus to improvement. The incentive scheme emerged as a topic of importance only as the preliminary investigation progressed.

Part of this consisted of individual interviews and group discussions, in groups of 3 people, with a total of 28 employees who were either paid on incentives or supervised an incentive paid section. For most of these people, the incentive scheme and its problems loomed large. Their comments were often forceful and had an emotional tone to them, which sometimes made it difficult to identify the exact points being made or the real nature of the grievance being expressed. Gradually, two themes began to emerge, each of which had been quite prominent in previous research into incentive systems.

The first of these problem areas was the frustration caused by the company's policy of continually retiming production standards. Any improvement in manufacturing methods or equipment resulted in a new standard being set. This meant that the individual operator, as he saw it, did not share in the improving efficiency of the factory. Personal gain from any improvements in methods which the individual operators might have developed tended to be lost in the consequent adjustment of rates.

The second type of criticism was that the incentive scheme did not make sense to its recipients, or was incomprehensible. Individuals mentioned particular aspects of the scheme which they had experienced or particular events which had occurred, which they found puzzling or confusing. The various adjustment and correction factors, and the rules governing their application, seemed a source of discontent. Supervisors responsible for incentive paid sections commented that they were frequently asked to explain points concerning the scheme. Their answers never satisfied those who raised the questions.

QUESTIONNAIRE DESIGN AND ANALYSIS

The analysis to be presented here concerns only the hourly-paid production workers who participated in the incentive payment system — this group was 126 strong. Multiple regression analysis and multiway table analysis were both inapplicable with such relatively limited data. An approximate method will be used in place of these multivariate techniques. This is to analyse a series of two-way sub-tables of the (hypothetical) multiway table; and to consider how far those sub-tables were consistent with the properties that one would (on the basis of theory) expect to find in the multiway table.

But it is not possible to develop an analogous method to replace the multiple regression analysis of *large* sets of variables. For a set of K variables, there are $\frac{1}{2}K(K-1)$ two-way sub-tables or correlation coefficients. So, as the number of variables considered increases, it rapidly becomes very cumbersome to review the two-variable relationships. Accordingly, no attempt will be made to analyse the complete range of employment attitudes in this survey. Instead, analysis will be concentrated upon attitudes to pay and to the administrative pay system.

Because of the findings in the preliminary discussions, it was decided to develop a number of special questions to represent the issues concerning incentive systems in the questionnaire. Eight questions were finally constructed and pre-tested on this theme. These are shown in Table 8.1, along with four further questions of a more general nature concerning pay, and one question again of a fairly general nature concerning personal experience of work pressure.

The general questions about pay were standard ones covering 'overall pay satisfaction', the satisfactoriness of external comparisons, of progress in individual earnings, and of the relationship of pay to effort.

The incentive pay system items were all specially constructed. Two reflected general feelings of satisfaction with the scheme. These looked at the scheme first in terms of a comparison process, relating to fairness of incentives between different groups of staff, and second in

TABLE 8.1. Wording of Attitude Items

Pay Items
1. On the whole my present earnings are fair.
2. I am satisfied with my progress in earnings since I joined the company.
3. Earnings in the plant are good compared with other companies in the area.
4. For the work I do my earnings are poor.
   (work pressure)
5. I am frequently under too much pressure in my job.

Incentive Items
1. The incentives favour some people more than others.
2. I do not understand the incentive plan.
3. Often I cannot tell what I have earned for the work I have done.
4. The incentive plan gives fair money for work done.
5. The company tries to maintain accurate standards.

Preferences regarding alternatives to existing scheme
6. I would prefer a system where everyone in the plant shared the same bonus.
7. I would prefer to earn an individual bonus.

terms of an effort–reward relationship. Next, two questions referred to the problem of understanding or confusion relating to the incentive system. The different emphases of the two items – one referring to understanding of the incentive scheme in absolute terms, the other referring to the more limited question of whether the individual was able to predict his pay – were guided by the findings of a study by Shimmin[1]. A further question asked whether the employee considered that the incentive standards were maintained in a fair manner. The question concerning work pressure was also thought to have some possible relationship to the question of incentive standards, as well as to effort and reward in general.

The final element of the subset of questions which we will be considering was a pair concerning preference for change in the incentive system. It seemed apparent enough from the interviews that some change in the system, or possibly the complete abolition of the incentive scheme, was desired by the majority of the incentive paid employees. With the benefit of hindsight, it might have been best to restrict the question to confirming this general desire for a change. However, this was considered unambitious, and an attempt was made to formulate

The Manufacturing Plant

definite alternatives in the direction of which employees might wish to move. There were a few comments in the interviews which suggested two directions of change. Some people, for instance, seemed to think that it was unfair that different grades of employees should receive different bonus rates and appeared to be suggesting a more egalitarian kind of scheme. Others seemed to be suggesting that a similar kind of individual scheme, but without group-related correction factors, would be easier to understand and more acceptable. Hence the two possibilities presented in the questionnaire. These two questions were also used as the criterion of conflict, since they were intended to reflect the will to act as opposed to mere dissatisfaction. The other criterion variable used was, as usual, the standard question concerning the 'overall satisfaction' of the employee.

THE QUESTIONNAIRE SURVEY

All the production employees, including those paid on the incentive plan, were given the opportunity of completing the questionnaire during their normal working hours and on company premises – either in a conference room or in the canteen. The shop stewards and local officials of the TGWU had also been informed of the survey, and although they did not actively encourage their members to complete questionnaires, they approved of the survey in principle. From 126 incentive paid workers, 118 usable questionnaires were obtained – a response rate of 94 per cent.

It may be helpful initially to present the simple descriptive results for each of the questions which will be used in the tests of hypotheses. These are shown in Table 8.2. There is a striking contrast between the results for some of the 'incentives' questions, and the results for the 'pay' questions and the 'overall satisfaction' question. Some 20 per cent of the incentive payment employees described themselves as dissatisfied with their employment, which is not at all an exceptional figure[2]. Similarly 55 per cent state that they are satisfied with their pay in overall terms, a figure which is again quite typical[3]. On the other hand, for 4 of the 7 incentive attitude questions the proportion giving a satisfied reply is in the range of 15–21 per cent. These 4 questions consist of the 2 most general questions concerning satisfaction with incentives, and the 2 questions concerning the understanding of incentives. The first impression therefore is that the incentive scheme is much more a focus for hostile feelings than pay in general.

TABLE 8.2. Descriptive Results from the Manufacturing Survey

	% giving favourable response
Pay Items	
1. Pay satisfaction	55
2. Pay progress	47
3. External pay comparisons	53
4. Pay for work	43
5. Work pressure	58
Incentive Items	
1. Incentives fair between workers	20
2. Understood incentive system	15
3. Understood incentive earnings	21
4. Incentives fair for work done	19
5. Standards accurate	52
6. Change to plant-wide scheme	42
7. Change to individual scheme	57
Overall Satisfaction	
Completely satisfied, very satisfied or satisfied	55
Neither satisfied nor dissatisfied	26
Dissatisfied, very dissatisfied or completely dissatisfied	19

TESTS OF HYPOTHESES

Hypotheses were expressed in a modified form in this case-survey, because only a small selected set of attitude items were analysed, rather than the complete range of employment attitudes. The results on which all the tests of hypotheses were based were a set of 78 two-by-two contingency tables. Although the statistical treatment was different in this case by comparison with the two previous cases, the process of reasoning required to test the hypotheses has been similar.

(a) *The Psychological Structure of Attitudes*

The 10 questionnaire items included in Table 8.3 have been divided into two groups: those which on the face of it relate to 'pay' or earnings, and those which relate more specifically to the 'incentive scheme'. Not included in this table are the criterion variables – relationships

TABLE 8.3. Associations: 'Pay' and 'Incentives' Variables

		'Pay'					'Incentives'			
		1	2	3	4	5	1	2	3	4
'Pay'										
Pay satisfaction	1									
Pay progress	2	38.09*								
External pay comparisons	3	17.69*	27.01*							
Pay for work	4	8.45*	14.68*	4.50*						
Work pressure	5	2.29	5.40*	3.17†	7.15*					
'Incentives'										
Incentives fair between workers	1	2.27	3.54†	0.00	5.60*	0.10				
Understood incentive system	2	0.09	1.01	0.00	1.98	2.63	9.47*			
Understood incentive earnings	3	0.61	2.69	0.38	4.56*	0.00	9.19*	29.62*		
Incentives fair for work done	4	8.83*	9.39*	8.91*	2.79	2.33	7.75*	1.66	2.33	
Standards accurate	5	2.08	1.72	0.82	1.36	3.97	0.25	0.02	0.65	4.60*

Each entry is a chi-square statistic on 1 *df*.
* Significant relationships.
† Approaching significance.

with these will be reported subsequently. The criterion variables are of two kinds, (i) the 'overall satisfaction' measures, and (ii) the 'potential conflict' measures, here represented by employees' wishes to change to a different kind of incentive scheme.

Looking at the upper triangle of relationships in Table 8.3, one will see that most of the 'pay' items are strongly related to one another (8 of the 10 coefficients are significant). They form a highly interconnected group. Similarly, looking at the bottom-right triangle of relationships in the table, one will see that there are many significant relationships among the 'incentives' items, although the relationships are less uniform than in the case of 'pay' (5 of the 10 coefficients were significant). If, however, one looks in the central rectangle of the table, which shows the relationships *between* the 'pay' items and the 'incentives' items, one will see that there are relatively few significant relationships (6 of the 25 coefficients were significant), and the three largest relationships were due to a single 'incentive' item.

Though the fine detail of the results requires more examination, this broad picture is sufficient to show that the 'pay' attitudes and the 'incentives' attitudes are genuinely distinct sets. Although there is a degree of relationship *between* the sets, there is much more relationship *within* each set. (This line of reasoning comes from Campbell and Fiske[4].) Also, the 'pay satisfaction' variable was strongly related to other 'pay' attitudes, but much less so to the 'incentives' attitudes.

TABLE 8.4. Associations with 'Overall Satisfaction'

(a) *Pay Attitudes*	
Pay satisfaction	8.77*
Pay progress	17.98*
External pay comparisons	7.65*
Pay for work	11.19*
Work pressure	10.03*
(b) *Incentives attitudes*	
Incentives fair between workers	2.56
Understood incentive system	0.56
Understood incentive earnings	3.25†
Incentives fair for work done	3.46†
Standards accurate	1.22

Each entry in the table is a chi-square statistic on 1 *df*.
* Highly significant.
† Approaching significance.

The Manufacturing Plant

Since the 'pay' attitudes are more general and the 'incentives' attitudes more detailed, this result is consistent with the hypothesis of hierarchical structure.

Another result which points in the same direction is summarised in Table 8.4. This is the different relationships that 'pay' and 'incentives' attitudes have to the 'overall satisfaction' criterion. The former generally have significant relationships while the latter do not. If one assumed that the 'pay' attitudes are at a higher level than the 'incentives' attitudes, this is the result that one would predict.

The distinctness of the 'pay' attitudes from the 'incentives' attitudes already suggests the presence of an attitude multistructure, but to test this more directly one needs to introduce the second type of criterion variable. The result of doing so is shown in Table 8.5, reporting the

TABLE 8.5. Associations Between Pay Attitudes and Preference for Change in Incentive System, and Between Incentives Attitudes and Preferences for Change in Incentive System

	Preference for change to plant-wide shared bonus system	Preference for change to completely individual bonus system
(a) Pay Attitudes		
Pay satisfaction	0.87	2.71
Pay progress	0.43	1.50
External pay comparisons	0.43	1.89
Pay for work	1.92	0.33
Work pressure	2.06	0.58
(b) Incentives Attitudes		
Incentives fair between workers	4.30*	0.75
Understand incentive system	4.26*	0.02
Understand incentive earnings	3.48†	0.09
Incentives fair for work done	0.20	0.53
Standards accurate	0.41	0.97

Each entry is a chi-square statistic on 1 df.
* Significant.
† Approaching significance.

relationships of the 'pay' and 'incentives' attitudes to each of the criterion variables concerning preference for a different kind of incentive scheme. One of these criterion variables turns out to be ineffective, since none of the attitude variables is significantly related to it. But with the other criterion variable, three of the 'incentives' attitudes are related, albeit moderately. However, none of the 'pay' attitudes are related in this way.

So, taking the evidence of Tables 8.4 and 8.5 together, one sees that whereas 'pay' attitudes are related to 'overall satisfaction' while 'incentives' attitudes are not, these roles are reversed when the criterion of conflict is introduced. The two kinds of attitudes form a dualistic structure.

(b) *The Meaning of Pay Attitudes*

The results for the 'pay' attitudes are recapitulated in Table 8.6. 'Pay satisfaction' is related to all the other pay attitudes, and the relationships are generally very significant. This broad basis of pay evaluations is consistent with the hypothesis of calculative rationalism, but inconsistent with the 'social relativist' position.

TABLE 8.6. Associations Between 'Pay' Variables

Label Pay satisfaction	1	*1*	*2*	*3*	*4*
Pay progress	2	38.09*			
External pay comparisons	3	17.69*	27.01*		
Pay for work	4	8.45*	14.68*	4.50*	
Work pressure	5	2.29	5.40*	3.17	7.15*

Each entry in the table is a chi-square statistic on 1 *df*.
* Significant relationships.

Another notable point is that, in spite of the prominence of the incentive scheme in the preliminary interviews, the 'pay for effort' item had if anything the least influence on the remaining pay attitudes. If the importance of the incentive scheme for workers was an economic one, this should have showed in an enhanced significance of the 'pay

The Manufacturing Plant

for effort' item – on the reasonable assumption that this, economically speaking, is what incentives are about.

In short, the pay attitudes present a picture which has already grown familiar in the two previously discussed case-surveys, and this picture is relatively unaffected by the strong feelings surrounding the incentive scheme.

(c) *Incentives and Conflict*

It has been seen that 'pay' attitudes are unrelated to the two items concerning preference for a change to different kinds of incentive system. Attention can be focused therefore on the 'incentive' items and their pattern of relationships with these criterion variables, shown in Table 8.5.

The criterion item yielding significant relations concerned preference for a shared plant-wide bonus scheme. Those employees who felt that the incentive scheme did not treat all workers fairly, and/or felt that they did not understand the scheme, were more likely to want a change to this other type of incentive scheme. As always it is important to consider the items where relationships did *not* emerge. Desire for a change of incentive scheme was *not* connected with feelings that the existing incentive scheme failed to give adequate money for work done, *nor* with adverse feelings about the incentive standards.

These results are not consistent with the hypothesis that it is the economic exchange relation embodied in the incentive scheme which is the source of hostility towards it. The results are consistent, though, with the hypothesis that the incentive scheme embodies authority relations, that these express themselves through feelings of confusion and of arbitrary treatment, and that from this source the desire for change arises. The justification for a single cohesive explanation is strengthened by the strong relationships which the three 'incentives' items concerned have with each other. This can be seen by referring to Table 8.7.

But why was there no similar pattern of relationships with the other criterion variable? One possible line of explanation is that although both the preference questions were indicators of the desire to change the incentive scheme, they had different significance for the employees because they were, so to speak, changes in opposite directions. Preference for an individual incentive scheme would, relative to the existing incentive scheme, have been a move towards stronger personal incentive rather than weaker. By contrast, preference for a plant-wide

112 The Hidden Meaning of Pay Conflict

TABLE 8.7. Association Between 'Incentives' Attitudes

Label		*1*	*2*	*3*	*4*
Incentives fair between workers	1				
Understood incentive system	2	9.47*			
Understood incentive earnings	3	9.18*	29.62*		
Incentives fair for work done	4	7.75*	1.66	2.33	
Standards accurate	5	0.25	0.02	0.65	4.60*

Each entry in the table is a chi-square statistic on 1 *df*.
* Significant relationships.

shared incentive scheme would have represented a fairly radical departure from the principle of an individual effort–reward bargain, and a move towards gain-sharing or productivity-sharing. The former type of scheme, one might imagine, clarifies the relationship between individual work and reward, but in doing so also tightens the control of the incentive scheme over the individual. The latter type of scheme makes the relationship between individual output and reward a more remote one, and thereby weakens the personal control factor in the incentive scheme.

CONCLUDING DISCUSSION

The description of the production plant at the outset of this chapter depicted an organisation which had reached a high pitch of efficiency. At the same time, by a policy of physical decentralisation into small units, and development of a clear personnel philosophy, the organisation had been able to maintain good personal relationships between management and workers – a fact that was directly verified by the survey. But while the managers and supervisors were not by any means seen as unduly authoritarian or oppressive in their style, the *system* of authority in the plant was a strong one. Workers had to operate under a strict discipline, formed from standards and procedures to which management, as much as themselves, were subject. The discipline enforced by the control systems was a rational and impersonal one, and since by rational standards the company was exceedingly successful, difficult to oppose on that score. Here is a situation in which the most important forms of authority in the organisation have taken on a most abstract and impersonal form.

The Manufacturing Plant

Of the various control systems comprising the authority structure, the most prominent and important for the ordinary production worker was likely to have been the incentive scheme. For, apart from affecting his actual remuneration, the incentive scheme was the channel through which both the methods and the prescribed pace of work were established. Furthermore, the effort which the company put into its incentive system, and the continual up-dating of standards which resulted, meant that the system was continuously in front of the worker's eyes.

How was the worker to express resistance to this incentive scheme? The technical expertise of the company in this area, its large, highly qualified, well trained staff of industrial engineers, and the complexity of the scheme itself, must have made it difficult for the individual employee to find loop-holes or 'buck the system'. The high status of the industrial engineers in this organisation, which was mentioned earlier, perhaps reflects the relatively strong power position they held compared to the shop-floor workers. In many parts of the industrial sub-culture of Britain, the industrial engineer – or rather, as he is normally called, the work study man – is stereotyped as a wretched figure of fun. Not so in this production plant. No group displayed, in the survey itself, higher levels of satisfaction.

Crozier's[5] suggestion of a margin of uncertainty around an already fixed system remains an illuminating one. For the complexity of the system itself, its technical incomprehensibility, presents to the worker exactly such a margin of uncertainty. Although perhaps convinced that the industrial engineer is honestly applying the rules of the scheme, the worker's inability to grasp the logic of that scheme, renders its effects on himself continuously unpredictable, and therefore in principle threatening. These feelings are confirmed and fed whenever he identifies examples of apparent anomalies in the payments arising to individuals from the incentive scheme: and these feelings can naturally be generalised into a criticism of the 'unfairness' of the scheme. It is thus the apparently *arbitrary* aspects of an intendedly rational scheme on which the worker focuses. And, in doing so, he begins to cast doubt on the very rationality on which the scheme is based. This is not at all a bad strategy for attacking the impersonal system of authority.

The importance of 'understanding' as a factor in the reactions of employees to incentive schemes has frequently been noted in other researches, such as those of Lawler[6], Shimmin[7], and of the Commission on Industrial Relations[8]. Yet, perhaps because it seems such a trivial cause for complaint, little attempt has been made to treat it seriously within the theory of conflict. The virtue of my explanation has been to show how theory *requires* trivial causes for certain cases of conflict.

One possible cause for complaint about the analysis which has been presented lies in the criterion variables for conflict. The mere expression of a desire for change of incentive scheme may be considered a weak and even a dubious sign of conflict. But, as I have emphasised, the choice and wording of survey items must be judged against the background provided by the preliminary investigation. During the course of the year following the survey, industrial disputes resulting in strike action of several weeks' duration took place both at the plant investigated in the present case survey and in a sister plant in another part of the country. It appears that the disputes arose from demands by the work force for the company to discontinue the incentive schemes. There is some justification from hindsight, therefore, for the way in which the issue of conflict has been handled in the design and analysis of this survey.

9 Summary and Implications

The purpose of the first part of this chapter is to draw together the main findings from the case-surveys presented in the three preceding chapters, to assess their cumulative evidence, and to state the main conclusions of the research. The characteristics of the organisational situations studied will also be discussed, in order to judge the scope and the limitations of the findings. In the second part of the chapter, a discussion of selected aspects of the findings will follow.

SUMMARY OF FINDINGS RELATING TO THE PSYCHOLOGICAL THEORY OF EMPLOYMENT ATTITUDES

The psychological theory proposed in Chapter 2 stated that employment attitudes constitute a 'hierarchical multistructure':

(a) The attitudes are arranged in various levels or layers of superordinate and subordinate relationships, hence they are hicrarchical.
(b) High-level superordinate attitudes tend to have different though possibly overlapping relationships with subordinate attitudes, to be divergent rather than convergent; hence the system of relations is a multistructure, not a unitary structure.
(c) A corollary to these two propositions is that superordinate attitudes are generally influenced by numerous subordinate attitudes: many-variable rather than 'one-to-one' relationships prevail.

Evidence for the Hierarchical-Attitude Hypothesis

The hypothesis that attitudes are hierarchically organised was tested in each of the three surveys. In two of these surveys – the hotels and finance company studies – it was tested in two different ways, while the third-survey – in the manufacturing plant – provided a single test. The basic approach was similar in all these tests. It was to divide up sets of attitude expressions into those that were on logical or linguistic grounds considered to be of a higher or superordinate level, and those that were of lower or subordinate levels. Either two or three levels of attitudes were distinguished in this way, for different purposes. Where three levels of attitudes were specified, a direct test of the assumption of hierarchical structure could be applied : the highest-level attitudes should be more strongly related to attitudes at the next or 'middle-range' level, than to attitudes at the lowest level.

In the hotels case-survey and the finance company case-survey, this kind of test was applied using a measure of 'overall satisfaction' as the high-level or superordinate variable, and sub-dividing the remaining attitudes about the employment situation into a smaller set of middle-range variables and a larger set of lower-level variables. It was found that, in both cases, most of the middle-range attitudes were highly related to overall satisfaction, while relatively few of the lower-level attitudes had substantial relationships. Confirmatory analyses showed that the middle-range variables *on their own* achieved a good level of fit when used to account for 'overall satisfaction'. The evidence of these analyses indicates that we have identified a hierarchical structure within employment attitudes.

Another three-level test of the hypothesis was provided, in all three case-surveys, by analyses of pay attitudes, rather than of employment attitudes as a whole. Here the high-level or superordinate attitude was taken to be an expression of the overall fairness of pay, or 'pay satisfaction' for short. Evaluations of various broad aspects of pay were taken as the next level, and attitudes concerning details of the pay systems as the lowest level. The results were in every case of a similar form. The broad evaluations of pay were highly related to 'pay satisfaction'. The more detailed pay systems attitudes, however, had in general much slighter relationships with 'pay satisfaction' though in some instances they had substantial relationships with one or more of the intermediate-level pay evaluations. These findings again indicate success in identifying a hierarchical structure within employment attitudes.

There is a second sense in which the analyses of pay attitudes support those of employment attitudes as a whole. For they show that hierarchical structure is not something generated only by the use of global measures such as 'overall satisfaction'. Rather, hierarchical structure can persist even within the attitudes concerning a relatively specific topic such as pay. The identification of hierarchical structure does not appear to depend on the choice of the highest level of attitudes in the analysis, but rather on having a sufficient depth of detail within the area being studied.

The conclusion from this aspect of the research is that the hypothesis of hierarchical structure is supported.

Evidence for the Hypothesis that Attitudes Form Multistructures

The idea incorporated in the 'multistructure' hypothesis is that an individual's attitudes do not constitute a unitary or monolithic system, even within a naturally occurring domain such as employment attitudes. Rather, the attitudes are combined by the individual in different ways as he looks upon his situation from different perspectives. In order to operationalise and test this notion, we distinguished on *a priori* grounds two broad perspectives used by individuals: that of 'evaluation' (or 'satisfaction') and that of 'future-attitudes'. In each of the three surveys the 'evaluation' perspective was expressed in terms of the 'overall satisfaction' measure. 'Future-attitudes' however, were expressed by different measures in each of the three surveys:

Hotels survey: measure of 'intention to leave or stay'.
Finance company survey: measure of 'support for union representation'.
Manufacturing plant : measure of 'preference for new pay system'.

The hypothesis for each survey was that the two types of criterion measured should depend upon or be explained by different (though perhaps somewhat overlapping) sets of attitudes.

In the hotels survey, a particularly clear test was obtained because it was possible to analyse both 'overall satisfaction' and 'intention to leave or stay' in an exactly parallel manner, using the same set of attitudes as explanatory variables. While two of the attitude variables proved to be important in both analyses, the remaining significant variables were different from one equation to the other. 'Overall satisfaction' was mainly related to a set of the 'middle-range' attitudes covering various broad aspects of the employment setting. But for 'intention to leave or stay' a group of attitudes concerned with details of the pay system became important, while most of the variables important in connection with 'overall satisfaction' now dropped out of the picture.

The finance company survey, for data analysis reasons, required a more complex and indirect approach, but the qualitative conclusion was a similar one. 'Overall satisfaction' was highly related to 'middle-range' attitudes; but a composite measure largely based on these was not a significant predictor of 'support for union representation'. However, another composite variable reflecting attitudes to recent changes in the company's personnel policies was significantly related to 'support for union representation'. Although the contrast somewhat oversimplifies the explanation of 'preference for union representation', a legitimate conclusion is that the latter had a quite different structure of subordinate attitudes from 'overall satisfaction'.

In the manufacturing plant survey, the analysis was relatively limited. It treated attitudes concerning pay only, not employment attitudes as a whole. However, the same kind of division was obtained among the pay attitudes as with the other two more extensive survey analyses. Attitudes towards broad aspects of pay were strongly associated with 'overall pay satisfaction' but not with the measure of 'preference for a new pay system'. Attitudes towards certain aspects of incentives – their comprehensibility, and their fairness of treatment of different workers – were significantly associated with 'preference for a new pay system', but not with 'overall pay satisfaction'.

The results of these three surveys, considered together, suggest that 'future-attitudes' of whatever kind have a different subordinate structure of attitudes from 'evaluations' or 'satisfaction'. This supports the more general notion of attitude domains as 'multistructures'.

Evidence for the Corollary of Many-variable Relationships

The notion of hierarchically organised attitude systems with multiple sub-structures implies the prevalence of many-to-one rather than one-to-one relationships among the attitudes. If, when one focused upon a particular attitude, one found that it was dominated by some other single attitude, this would weaken the support for the theory of attitude structure.

It is not necessary to review the evidence for this aspect of the theory in detail. Suffice to say that, in all the main analyses conducted in each of the three surveys there were numerous attitudes involved in explanatory relationships. There was no case where the dependent variable of interest could be accounted for exclusively by the action of

Summary and Implications 119

one or two other attitudes. This was true even if one considered only direct influences, but in addition there were often numerous indirect influences. This was because of the tendency of the attitudes to form hierarchical networks. There is therefore nothing inconsistent in any of the case-surveys with the corollary of many-variable relationships.

SUMMARY OF FINDINGS RELATING TO THE SOCIOLOGICAL THEORY OF PAY ATTITUDES AND CONFLICT

The sociological or substantive theory of pay attitudes, set out in Chapters 3 and 4, stated that they are essentially a duality. Pay mediates both economic relationships and authority relationships; and it is because of the latter role that it becomes a focus for organisational conflict. Pay attitudes partly reflect an economically rational orientation, but in part they reflect the employees' degree of opposition to the authoritarian control inherent in payment systems. It should be possible to test this formulation, therefore, by identifying two distinct patterns of relationships among pay attitudes, corresponding to these two underlying social relationships.

The Economic Rationality of Pay Evaluations

The hypothesis advanced was that economic rationality constituted the dominant orientation when employees made overall evaluations concerning the satisfactoriness or fairness of their pay. This hypothesis could be tested if one could distinguish it from alternatives and state the characteristic attitude relationships expected under each theoretical position. The contrast developed was between economic rationalism as an explanation of pay evaluations, and 'social relativism' as a competing explanation. Two hallmarks of economic rationality were noted by means of this contrast: first, the dependence of pay evaluations on a wide and balanced set of attitudes towards various aspects of pay; and second, the inclusion among these aspects of some that were 'self-referent', based on comparisons with one's own experience rather than on comparisons with other groups of workers.

The finance company survey and the hotels survey both provided clear tests of the hypothesis, and the results in each case were similar. Overall pay satisfaction depended on a range of subsidiary evaluations, with no one or two of these being dominant. Moreover, the aspects which proved significant included attitudes towards pay progression, towards payment for effort expended or for responsibility assumed, and towards the cost-of-living element in pay: these aspects may all be interpreted without strain as 'self-referent'.

The results of these two surveys also directly contradicted the use of 'group-referent' interpretations. Attitudes towards pay comparisons with others, both within and outside the place of employment, were included in multivariate analyses. If they provided the true explanation of pay satisfaction, then they should have dominated the relationships and suppressed the effects of the other pay attitudes on pay satisfaction. They did not do so, but contributed moderately to the overall explanation along with the other influential pay attitudes.

The manufacturing plant survey, because of its smaller size, was analysed in a more limited way. Nevertheless its results were consistent with those of the other two surveys, and it is natural to interpret them in the same way.

The conclusion is that an interpretation based on economic rationality is adequate to explain the survey results, while a social-relativistic explanation is not sufficient to account for them.

Attitudes to Pay Systems and Conflicts

Evidence was obtained concerning four propositions, which support the notion that pay systems are a focus of conflict, and that this arises because they express authority relations. The propositions are:

1. Issues of authority and power are involved in the pay system.
2. Attitudes to aspects of the pay system which involve these issues of authority and power, are also related to independent measures of readiness for conflict.
3. Attitudes to pay systems, even when they are significant predictors of readiness for conflict, are not strongly related to overall pay evaluations.
4. Overall pay evaluations are not predictors of readiness for conflict.

The evidence that issues of authority and power were involved in the pay systems came from the preliminary background investigations of the case-surveys, and was of a qualitative type. In the hotels, there was a tradition of managerial autocracy, and while the managers in the hotel company studied were generally facing a reduction in the scope

Summary and Implications 121

of their powers, they were able to use the pay system to reassert those powers in a number of ways. They had discretion over individual pay increases, over the rules for overtime payment, and especially over the distribution of rewards from the 'service charge' system; they exercised this discretion in a way which made employees conscious of it. In the finance company, the personal nature of managerial authority was no longer to the fore, but impersonal and formalised control had been increased through a programme of change in personnel policies. Aspects of the pay system, especially job grading, appraisal and merit awards, played a central role in this bureaucratisation of relationships between employer and employee. The third study, in the manufacturing plant, concerned an incentive payment system which evidently functioned as the main instrument of control over the work force. This complex and unyielding system created reactions of confusion and frustration in many of the incentive-paid workers.

The measures of conflict were different in each situation. Problems of high labour turnover in the hotel industry and the difficulty for hotel employees of expressing opposition except through leaving their employment, suggested that this would be an appropriate criterion in this case. In the finance company, the recent development of white-collar unionism provided the obvious opportunity for measuring conflict, through individuals' support for unionisation. In the manufacturing plant, conflict was evidently developing beneath a surface of stability, but it was less obvious how it should be revealed. The approach used was to ask the employees whether they would prefer an alternative type of incentive system, thus providing some indication of the developing pressure towards change.

In each of the surveys, aspects of the payment system which had been interpreted in terms of authority and power relations were generally related as hypothesised to the criteria of conflict. Although there were exceptions to this generalisation, and although the magnitude of the relationships was in some cases modest, the results of the three studies were mutually supportive. The attitudes to pay systems that were connected to the criteria of conflict were *not*, however, good predictors of satisfaction with pay as a whole: this again is as predicted.

Moreover, in none of the surveys was there any evidence that employees' general satisfaction with their pay contributed to their readiness for conflict. This lack of effect, predicted by the theory, was in various ways surprising from a naive common-sense viewpoint. In the hotels, the prevailing low levels of pay might have been expected to stimulate dissatisfaction with pay and hence leaving intentions. In the finance company, satisfaction with pay was one of the most important factors in overall satisfaction, and conversely one might have expected that dissatisfaction with pay would be important in fostering unionism. In the manufacturing plant, the incentive scheme constituted an important element of total earnings, and the conflict over incentives might plausibly have had a purely economic motivation. The absence of effects in all these situations throws into relief the significant relationships between attitudes to payment *systems* and readiness for conflict.

Thus all the four types of evidence considered support the view that attitudes to pay systems are a focus of conflict; and that this arises because the pay systems mediate relationships of authority and power.

THE SCOPE OF THE FINDINGS

The findings from the case-surveys have consistently supported the theories which have been proposed. A question which one should consider, however, is whether this outcome has been influenced by the types of situation studied. The support for the theories will be greater if the evidence comes from widely different studies, and it will be less if the studies are of a narrowly limited type.

In a number of simple ways, the organisations studied in the three cases differed substantially from one another. The main and most obvious differences were in the following respects:

Industry

The companies belonged to industrial sectors which are generally regarded as distinct: the hotel and catering sector, the banking and financial services sector, and the general manufacturing sector. This broad distinction naturally incorporates many subsidiary ones, which we will not attempt to enumerate.

Nature of Work and Labour Markets

The type of work characteristic of each company differed and, accordingly, so did the labour markets from which workers were drawn. The finance company provided exclusively white-collar office occupations, and drew its work force from clerical and professional groups.

Summary and Implications

The manufacturing plant provided industrial process and machining jobs, and employed mainly semi-skilled manual workers. Hotel jobs often fit uneasily into either manual or non-manual classes, so hotel workers may in some respects be considered intermediate between the two.

Stage of Organisational Development

The three companies differed clearly in the degree to which they had developed a bureaucratic form of organisation. Evidence for this distinction between them comes mainly from their personnel policies, since this was the main field of investigation, but there is little doubt that other aspects of their organisations followed a similar pattern. The hotel company was the least formalised in its personnel policies; much was left to the discretion of the local manager, and the methods used were often rough and ready. The finance company, after a history of indulgent paternalism, had recently passed through a programme of deliberate formalisation of personnel policy, combined with the introduction of professional personnel management. The manufacturing plant was part of a large organisation with managerial practices emphasising standardisation, technical efficiency and control in all spheres, including that of personnel.

Degree of Unionisation

The hotel workers showed no signs of unionisation (though doubtless there was some latent membership); the finance company was involved in a rapid first development of unionisation; and the manufacturing plant was fully unionised. Thus the degree of unionisation corresponded to the degree of formalisation of the three organisations.

Type and Complexity of Payment Systems

The differing payment systems in the three companies when ranked in order of complexity correspond once more to the degree of formalisation of the organisation. Each also had some distinct features. The service charge system in hotels, and the influence of 'tipping', had no parallel in the other two industries. The finance company alone had adopted performance appraisal and merit reviews of salary. Time-studied incentive schemes were the dominant features of pay in the manufacturing plant but did not occur in the other two examples.

However, the three companies *were* similar to one another in two respects which are generally considered important: their *sizes* and their *ownership*. All were large, and all were limited liability companies in the private sector. These points of similarity cannot detract from the importance of the distinctions to which attention has been drawn. It seems reasonable to conclude that the case-surveys were not replicas of one another and provided essentially distinct tests of the theory.

Partly as a result of the differences in the situations concerned, different operational variables were used to represent and test the theory. This has been another aspect of the scope of the research. Attitudes reflecting situationally specific aspects were used in all three surveys, and form a part of all the analyses reported. The results of the research have therefore not been dependent on a restricted or standardised set of attitude measures, nor upon a single specification of the variables of the payment system, nor upon a single measure of conflict.

FURTHER DISCUSSION OF RESEARCH FINDINGS

In the remainder of this chapter, I discuss the research findings in order to clarify their contribution to the study of the problems in question, and to point out some further implications. Each main aspect of the research is the subject of a separate brief discussion.

The Psychology of Employment Attitudes

The initial ideas for this research came from experimental psychology. In Chapter 2 a particular debt was acknowledged to the concepts and theories of Fishbein and Dulany. The main contribution of the research from a psychological viewpoint has consisted simply in the application of these ideas to the naturally occurring domain of employment attitudes.

By demonstrating that concepts from these general theories can fruitfully be transplanted to an applied field, one has strengthened confidence in their practical relevance. Conversely, by showing that employment attitudes can be handled within general notions of verbal behaviour and attitude formation, one has reduced the justification for a separate or special theory in this field. Whereas much research in employment attitudes has relied on motivational concepts and assumptions – drawn from theories which in themselves often have little experimental support – here one has developed hypotheses using only structural concepts, drawn from theories which have substantial experimental support.

In some respects, the research had enabled the general concepts with which it began to be expressed and tested in a more direct form than hitherto. This is true both of the notion of 'attitude hierarchy' and of the notion of 'attitude multistructure'. Because employment attitudes present such an extensive structure of relationships, and because two of the surveys provided large numbers of respondents, it was possible to develop operational hypotheses concerning these concepts, and to test them directly by multivariate analysis methods. These methods of testing structural hypotheses might be applied to other aspects of cognitive structure. The study of cognitive structure, which has so far been chiefly pursued by experimental psychologists, might be advanced by the increased use of survey methods, which can derive an advantage from naturally occurring complexity.

Employment Attitudes as Systems

A concept introduced in this research, which is not included in the theories of Dulany or Fishbein, is that of psychological 'systems' of employment attitudes. In part, this concept of attitude systems can be justified simply as a convenient descriptive label. It is a shorthand for structural characteristics which were used in the hypotheses, and these characteristics as we have seen can each be investigated in a direct manner. The use of the term therefore avoids the strictures of some critics[1] against untestable and overgeneralised use of 'systems theories'. In this research the concept has had a well defined and limited sense.

However, the notion of 'attitude systems' has some wider implications, if one looks beyond the problems considered here. It becomes particularly interesting where the dynamic 'behaviour' of the system in question displays properties which cannot be detected in the elements of the system by themselves. It is worth considering what are likely to be the dynamic characteristics of a system of employment attitudes which is a 'hierarchical multistructure'.

One important implication of such a system is that, the greater the number of attitudes involved in subordinate relationships within the system, the more stable is the behaviour of superordinate attitudes. Expressions of overall satisfaction with employment, or other general evaluations of the employment situation, are likely to display stability for this reason. Indeed, the evidence of the case-surveys suggests that such overall evaluations may be influenced by a remarkably large number of subordinate or more detailed attitudes. In such a system, one can expect that any *single* change in the situation, however drastic it may appear to be, will have only a slight influence on the employees' overall outlook, since this depends also on an extensive hierarchy of other attitudes.

Social psychologists have been primarily interested in attitude change rather than attitude stability; they seem to have made the assumption that attitudes are malleable. If, however, one assumes a high degree of stability in people's broad evaluative outlook, then the realistic measurement of major attitude change demands either longitudinal studies over substantial timespans or the study of attitudes under extreme conditions of social disruption.

Systematic evidence to test the prediction of employment attitude stability is not available, but some *ad hoc* comparisons may be drawn. A recent review of subjective social indicators[2] included American Gallup Poll data on a general 'job satisfaction' measure gathered since the Second World War. A feature of the results was the steady but *gradual* decline in satisfaction in the latter 1960s and early 1970s – so slow as to be insignificant if comparing adjacent years. The same review also presents longitudinal information for a selected group, American chemical engineers, and here the level of satisfaction expressed has been virtually unchanging. This circumstantial evidence concerning the stability of certain employment attitudes might be interpreted by further application of systems concepts.

A major contribution of systems theorists has been in suggesting that the properties of biological and psychological systems have adaptive value for the individual[3]. They can often be interpreted as means of coping with a changing environment. The stability of the individual's general evaluative framework in relation to his employment could be interpreted as an instance of psychological adaptation. The characteristics of the attitude system enable the individual to perceive detailed changes in his situation, to be sensitive to reality, without major disturbance of his overall evaluative outlook. If high-level evaluations were easily reversed, the individual would indeed have an 'unstable' or 'unpredictable' turn of mind, and would lack a firm sense of his life's condition. Alternatively, to maintain stability he would frequently have to deny reality or systematically distort the information he received in order to maintain consistency. It is indeed notions such as these which have been involved in the work of the 'cognitive dissonance' theorists[4].

In the domain of employment attitudes, however, because of the characteristics which I have demonstrated, there is likely to be relatively little pressure for internal cognitive consistency. A multilevel many-variable system can absorb a substantial degree of local inconsistency while maintaining a stable and predictable overall orientation.

The 'multistructure' characteristic of the employment attitude system enables this reasoning to be carried further. Not only is the stability of high-level evaluations safeguarded by the system's structure, but also this stability does not interfere with outputs of the system which need to be more responsive. Various superordinate attitudes can be largely (though not completely) independent of one another. For example – as we have shown – general evaluations of the employment situation may remain positive or favourable, without preventing the development of a rapid response to particular threats or pressures in the situation. The evaluation results from a process of wide-ranging aggregation, the reaction results from a process of selection. Even though the same domain of attitudes serves both, the former may remain stable though the direction of the latter is reversed.

It seems, therefore, that a system of attitudes as conceptualised in this theory not only conveniently describes the structural characteristics which have been investigated here but also acts as a bridge with other possible types of investigation. In particular, it shows the possibilities of investigating changes in employment attitudes over longer periods of time than are usually considered in applied social research.

Satisfaction and Action

We may now reconsider the much-debated question of the relationship between satisfaction and work behaviour. We have shown that expressions of satisfaction, both in principle and in practice, are distinct from 'future-attitudes', that is attitudes to future actions. In other words, satisfaction is distinct even from verbal surrogates of action. Therefore, it seems reasonable to predict *a fortiori* that satisfaction (or high-level evaluations in general) will be distinct from most forms of intentional action.

This should not be regarded as a paradox, but as an appropriate way for the cognitive system to function. For it would be a poor system which initiated action only in response to signals from its highest level, or which changed its course of action only when there were changes of its overall state. Action is better controlled by lower levels of the system, which are closer to the details of the situation and can respond appropriately to them. Only in some situation of crisis need the higher evaluative states become directly involved in determining action.

On this view, the problem of predicting action from employment attitudes becomes a much more intractable one for psychology. If changes in work behaviour are not associated with changes in satisfaction, how are they to be explained? Clearly some principle of *selection* from the set of employment attitudes must be involved, but it is hard to see how a psychological principle could make particular attitudes more relevant to action. The argument we have put forward is that, roughly speaking, the meaning of action is socially defined, and therefore, the attitudes which influence action can only be identified by analysing the social situation in which they arise. Attitudes-in-general cannot predict action-in-particular; and it is impossible to specify the particular attitudes which are relevant without consideration of specific issues and settings. Thus the problem of predicting action from attitudes inevitably leads across the border from psychology into sociology.

The Social Significance of Attitudes to Pay

The theory of attitudes to pay has been a sociological one, being based on analysing the *organisational context of pay*. Attitudes to pay, I have proposed, fall into two largely distinct groups, requiring different interpretations. This is because pay expresses both economic relationships and authority relationships in industrial organisations, and attitudes to pay reflect this real distinction.

In one branch of this theory, I have asserted the value of notions of economic rationality. The main contribution made by the present research has been in defining the characteristics of economically rational attitudes specifically with reference to pay; in predicting that these characteristics primarily apply to general evaluations of pay; and in developing contrasts between the economically rational interpretation and an alternative type of interpretation, labelled 'social relativism'. As a result of these steps, it has been possible not only to use notions of economic rationality in an interpretive way, but to conduct direct tests of hypotheses based on these interpretations.

The value of this type of analysis has been most apparent in the comparison between economic rationality and 'social relativism'. Debates concerning the validity of such concepts are frequently conducted in general and inconclusive terms. In the relatively limited field

Summary and Implications

of pay attitudes, it has been possible to derive specific applications of the abstract concepts, and to identify differences in the predictions which they generate, leading to conclusive tests. It remains possible of course for a critic to take issue with the way in which the concepts have been applied and redefined in the course of this process. But it would be reasonable to ask such a critic to specify alternative definitions which would also lead to decisive comparisons. In this way the issues may be kept within reach of empirical investigation.

Though economic rationality adequately explains evaluative attitudes to pay, it is – we have argued – divorced from issues of conflict. This is the part of the theory which contrasts most sharply with received notions, and has the greatest implications. To put these implications into perspective, it may be useful to follow the steps by which the theory has advanced. The theory, though distinct from previous accounts of conflict over pay, accords with a number of simple observations. Workers who evaluate themselves as well paid, as materially satisfied, do not for that reason opt out of industrial conflict. Among manual workers, groups regarded as élites are in many instances well known for their willingness to take industrial action. Again, times when payment systems are changing are specially prone to conflict, even though the changes may hold out promise of increased earnings for those affected.

The method of analysing attitudes which has been developed in this research has enabled these observations of experience to be formalised and submitted to direct test. It has been shown that pay satisfaction or dissatisfaction does not explain the role of pay in conflict. But this negative finding in itself would be inconclusive. A further concept is required, linking attitudes to pay and attitudes which express conflict. This linking concept, in our theory, is authority. The interpretation proposed has been that pay is a focus of conflict *because it mediates authority relations*.

However, authority is not a directly measured factor in our theory: it is an *interpretation* supported by qualitative observations and general arguments. The simpler, more immediately empirical fact, on which the interpretation has been based, is the prevalence of conflict over those aspects of pay which concern its function as a control system. Why, then, have I not used 'control' as the explanatory concept, rather than 'authority'?

The concept of authority has been preferred partly because control by itself appears to be an ambiguous concept, the meaning of which depends on – among other things – whether or not it is exercised within an authority relationship. Control appears to lead, logically, back to authority. Authority is also a more powerful concept because of its position in organisation theory and, especially, the theory of bureaucracy. By applying it in the field of pay, I have therefore been illustrating by specific example a more general problem of the modern organisation where authority is legitimated on rational grounds. Pay, with its apparently rational and economic basis, provides a natural opportunity for managerial authority to extend the scope of its control. Yet in developing pay as a control system, management calls into question the rationality of pay itself, and makes it the arena in which its authority may be opposed. Thus the theory of pay which I have developed is consistent with, and supports, Weber's more general analysis of the contradictions of authority in a capitalist society.

A further reason – and perhaps the most important – for preferring the notion of authority to the more limited one of control, lies in the policy implications which the larger concept evokes. Once one has established the relevance of the concept, within the research data, one may legitimately consider what further possibilities it contains. Here the richness of the concept of authority gives it a great advantage. Authority is closely bound up with the function of management, and with relations between management and workers which are of profound practical concern. By explicitly analysing the authority relations inherent in pay systems it is possible to reassess the worth of those systems and to consider new principles for their design. Also, because both authority relations and pay are important in the wider society, and are not confined to the context of organisations, the analysis proposed here might be applied to industry-wide or national problems of conflict over pay. An explicit analysis of authority relations has been lacking in discussions of national pay policy, and might well be introduced. It becomes apparent that implications are indeed both numerous and radical, extending far beyond what it would be reasonable to discuss in this account of research. I shall, however, briefly speculate on some of these implications in the next, and final, chapter.

10 The Problem of Authority

The previous chapter considered possible extensions, in theory and research, of the ideas that I have put forward. This chapter will consider possible extensions and applications in the practical area of pay system administration and design.

The process of research which preceded this book reflected the belief that pay was sufficiently important to demand the most fundamental analysis of which I was capable. But theory-building and testing does not complete this process. It has to be carried over into soundly based and effective practice, or else the original reason for studying the field is denied.

It would be pleasing to report that methods of applying the lessons of the research were well developed and proven. But that is not yet the case. The notion that pay is a matter of authority relations as well as of economic relations constitutes a radical change of viewpoint relative to the unquestioned assumptions of current practice. To apply this idea requires new problem-solving approaches, new design principles, and methods or processes of persuasion and change through which the resulting solutions can win acceptance. This chapter will offer only some initial, unsystematic efforts at such developments. However, provided that the chapter is viewed as a set of suggestions and sketches for further work, rather than as a set of final recommendations, it may still serve a useful purpose.

THINKING ABOUT PAY PROBLEMS

Stresses and tensions around payment systems are common and widespread. It would be impractical to suggest that all such situations require to be researched in depth before any diagnosis of the problems can be formed. Managers and worker representatives will in most of these cases lack the resources for such investigations, and will have to rely on their intuitive assessment of the situation. One of the main uses of a theory is in supplying fresh ways of thinking about problems. But to be useful in this way, the theory must achieve a natural fit with experience, and provide concepts which can readily be applied to a wide range of situations.

I began to test the potential of the theory in this respect by introducing the case-survey findings in study-group discussions with groups of managers. I usually presented these findings without any preliminary discussion of theory – merely as a set of results needing interpretation. However, I gave an orientation to the discussion by stressing the separation of the influences into two groupings, and suggesting that this was worth thinking about. In some instances, two influence diagrams from quite different situations were presented together – with the implication that they had something in common in spite of superficial appearances.

I found that managers rapidly accepted the notion that people's feelings about pay tended to split into two parts. They also readily agreed that since one of these parts was to do with the economic or 'money' aspects of pay, the other was in some way non-economic. Rather a wide variety of explanatory concepts were produced by different groups, such as anxiety, pressure, insecurity, suspicion and mistrust. These all appear to be subsidiary aspects of the general concepts of authority and power.

The experience of the discussion groups has also encouraged the belief that the dualistic or two-aspect analysis of pay attitudes can be applied to many situations of current interest. Since the groups were composed of managers, it was not surprising that they particularly transferred the notions to their experiences of salary systems. An especially common experience was with the introduction of job-evaluated salary scales[1]. The managers who had gone through this change had often felt confusing reactions in themselves. On the one hand, they liked the clarity and order of the scheme, and in many instances the removal of anomalies had resulted in higher salaries being paid. But they also felt 'regimented', 'boxed in', or 'made one of the herd' by such a development. If one accepted that such personal experiences were likely to have been part of a widespread reaction, it became easy to understand why such schemes (apparently installed to provide fair treatment of all salaried staff) should have been met by a barrage of criticism and obstruction. A margin of discretion which one could use to one's own advantage is not easily surrendered.

The Problem of Authority

To illustrate further how the two-aspect theory of pay can be applied, I will briefly discuss several other examples, considering evidence about the problems encountered and interpreting these problems in the light of the theory.

(a) Measured Daywork

Some manufacturing companies experiencing problems with conventional incentive bonus systems have replaced them by measured daywork schemes[2]. In these, work measurement is applied in the usual way to determine standards, but the variable incentive element of pay is replaced by a fixed high rate which the worker obtains by contracting to work at a fixed high output level. Firms expected that this type of scheme would help to eliminate much of the antagonism and uncontrollability of conventional incentives. But in practice several difficulties have been commonly encountered.

Although workers and their representatives often attack traditional incentives on the grounds of earnings fluctuations, the opportunity to switch to high fixed earnings has nevertheless been resisted. It is now widely recognised[3] that the main reason for this is the relative transfer of control over the work place from workers and shop stewards to management. This reaction would be predicted by the two-aspect theory; and the theory would also predict that this opposition to measured daywork would be independent of the financial gains involved, and dependent only on the state of authority and power relationships before and after the installation of the new system.

It has also been observed that the operational problems of measured daywork tend to focus upon first-line supervisors[4]. In measured daywork, the supervisor generally is required to control production to a greater degree and more directly. Since this amounts to a change in authority relationships, the theory would predict it to be a focus for conflict.

(b) Management-by-Objectives

In the past decade, a group of ideas known as 'management-by-objectives'[5] has come into wide use by large companies. Many organisations have used this approach not only as an aid to business planning and improvement, but also as a method of appraising the performance of individual managers and thus (directly or indirectly) of rewarding them.

Although initially hailed as a major improvement in management development, management-by-objectives has subsequently been shown to lead to many difficulties[6]. These include the resentment of managers towards increased pressure and manipulation; particularly when objectives are set without the participation of individual managers. Another factor causing problems is the feeling that significant aspects of management work are excluded from consideration within the mechanistic and inflexible setting of targets. Conversely, when firms have attempted to operate the method in a flexible and open way, the scheme has sometimes become a morass of bargaining and compromise.

These difficulties can readily be interpreted in the light of the two-aspect theory of pay. Management-by-objectives can be regarded as a further extension of the process of formalisation and bureaucratic control, illustrated in the finance company case study (Chapter 7). Unless introduced with great care, it may have the effect of reducing the manager's freedom to define his work for himself and to present a case in his own terms for promotion or salary increase. The incorporation of these elements into a system defined at a higher level in the organisation inevitably changes authority relationships in a manner which is threatening to all but the strongest individuals.

(c) *Salary Secrecy*

Secrecy is a customary feature of salary systems, even though open publication of manual wage rates has long been established. Whether this reduces the effectiveness of salary rewards, from a motivational viewpoint, has been particularly discussed by Lawler[7] and by Porter and Lawler[8]. The contention is that, unless there is a clear relationship between salary increases or differentials and the conditions on which they are contingent, then their effect in influencing work behaviour will be reduced.

Until recently, however, there has been little evidence that salary secrecy was resented or disliked by staff or managers. If one looks at secrecy as an aspect of authority or power relationships, rather than in motivational terms, one can see that under some circumstances it can be *favourably* received. It can form part of the 'particularism' of treatment given to relatively privileged members of an organisation, which creates a special bond between them and higher authority. The secrecy protects their own privileges from attack, as much as it prevents them from questioning the privileges of their peers or seniors.

But when particularism is replaced by formalised, systematic approaches to salary and other aspects of the treatment of staff, the significance of secrecy changes radically. The individual's progression is now controlled by a system which represents the organisation's authority over him, and is inimical to the notion of personal favour. Secrecy merely makes the system more impregnable to individual questioning or objection, and offers no compensating advantages.

I have recently been able to confirm this analysis in a small survey, the results of which are as yet unpublished. The survey took place after the introduction of a Hay–MSL salary scheme[9] for managers and senior staff. The company had witheld information about the basis for evaluating jobs in the scheme, and it had not been revealed where individuals had been placed on the scale of personal performance. These aspects of secrecy were the object of intense hostility, similar in many respects to the feelings expressed about 'not understanding the incentive scheme' in the manufacturing plant study described in Chapter 8. Informal discussions with managers from many other companies have suggested that this situation occurs wherever formalised salary structures are introduced without disclosing the rules and administrative practices involved. It is likely, in fact, that this kind of development serves to stimulate staff and management unionism.

(d) *Government Intervention*

The outstanding current example of changing relationships in the field of pay is greater intervention by the government in the processes of collective bargaining, especially in state-owned industries. An historical analysis of this recent trend has been provided by Hawkins in his account of the development of national disputes in the coal-mining industry[10]. Hawkins interprets the National Union of Mineworkers' strategy of using their power in a more forceful manner as a learned response to the previous use of power by successive governments in controlling pay awards. Indeed, Hawkins argues, governments not only made increased use of their own power in the industrial sphere, but they increasingly showed that they were primarily influenced by exhibitions of power by unions or pressure-groups. Unions therefore had to reinterpret the most effective way to deploy their own power.

Such a point has deep implications. The situation is likely to become unstable as the traditional boundaries for the use of power disappear. And in the second place, the conflict between employer and union now takes on a wider political significance, thereby breaking down the 'institutional isolation of conflict' of which Dahrendorf has spoken[11].

It is not surprising if the individual employee or group of employees feels profoundly threatened both by the development of a new source of overriding domination in the pay situation, and by the discarding of all the old rules and understandings.

These comments apply primarily to state industries, and a more complex and subtle effect is felt in the private sector. Workers in companies still deal directly with their employees on pay matters, not with the government. They cannot be in conflict with the government because no authority relationship is understood there. If they have a quarrel it will be with the management as usual. And many managements, thinking that in a period of government pay controls they would be absolved from blame, have been distressed to find that it has not turned out like that. The fact that the company controls dealings with government departments; that it is the main channel of communication on pay matters; and that it still has a margin of discretion, even in the most stringent 'pay freeze' – all these mean that, in employees' eyes, it retains authority over pay.

So, in a survey conducted at the end of 1976 (two years into the period of government pay policy), I found that most workers in a manufacturing plant continued to criticise the company rather than the government. In this particular case, most of the criticisms fell upon the company's job evaluation and job grading systems. The constraining effect of government pay restrictions on the administration of these systems was mostly ignored; those who referred to this, generally felt that the company used the government's pay policy as a pretext, as 'something to hide behind'. And, as the two-aspect theory of pay predicts, such criticisms were as likely to come from those who were satisfied with their earnings as from those who were dissatisfied.

I hope that these examples will be sufficient to indicate the potential of the two-aspect theory to interpret and to predict varied and unexpected problems of pay. I invite the reader to consider examples from his own experience, where problems of pay have either led to conflict, or at least aroused strong feelings. By thinking about the aspects of authority and power involved in those situations, I am confident that he will usually be able to obtain an improved intuition of the forces at work.

THE DESIGN OF PAYMENT SYSTEMS

So far I have talked about understanding or foreseeing pay problems. Is it possible to go further; to develop payment systems which will be

The Problem of Authority 137

less prone to conflict? In answering this question, one will be considering principles for the design of payment systems, and criteria for choosing between alternative design principles.

Existing techniques for analysis and choice in payment system design are formulated without questioning the framework of authority relations. This is not intended as a criticism: part of their usefulness consists in their close contact with these realistic constraints. But this framework naturally imposes limitations on what is considered. The techniques aim at finding decisions within an accepted range of possibilities, and of adjusting or modifying controls to cope with (among other things) prevailing norms of conflict. The elimination of conflict is not in itself a design objective. This is true even of the most sophisticated approaches to the evaluation and design of payment systems, such as those advanced by Lupton and Bowey[12].

My approach connects conflict with authority relations, and gives both a fundamental place in pay design. If the crucial problem is to reduce levels of conflict which are already dangerously high, then attention must be turned to the authority relations which underlie payment systems, and not be confined to the payment systems themselves. It is this thought which suggests the need for innovation in the underlying framework of authority, rather than continuing adjustments within fixed horizons.

Authority is an intrinsic part of industrial organisation; but the forms of relationship involved may not be completely inflexible. To borrow a phrase originally coined to counter technological determinism[13], there may be a degree of 'organisational choice' available concerning the use of authority in the design of pay systems.

A relevant contribution is Fox's recent elaboration of the concept of 'trust', with its contrast between high-trust and low-trust relations in industry[14]. Adapting a definition proposed by Zand[15], Fox suggests that trust is expressed when someone deliberately puts himself within the power of another party. This definition enables one to shake loose of the notion of trust as a sentiment or expression of personal regard, and to consider it as a structural relation. In this sense, trust or mistrust may often be written into the roles which people have to play. As Fox points out, one sometimes has no choice in the matter; trust – putting oneself in another's power – is inevitable, as in the case of the patient undergoing surgery. It is particularly significant that trust may be defined in terms of power relations, since this connects it with the two-aspect theory of pay.

Fox's suggestion is that where high trust is expressed, it tends to be reciprocated, and a situation develops in which power is neither exploited nor countered by conflict. Where low trust prevails, leading to high levels of conflict, the problem is to identify policies which allow high-trust relationships to develop. From a policy viewpoint, therefore, it may be worth examining the existing authority structure and power relations surrounding matters of pay determination, before considering the pay system itself. The possibility of permanently reducing pay conflict may depend upon the degree of innovation attainable in authority and power, and especially the possibilities for high-trust relationships.

It is possible that a far greater degree of participation could be granted to workers and their representatives in the design and administration of payment systems. Some possible mechanisms for developing and maintaining worker participation in this area have been suggested by Cliquet and Dumont[16]. It may however be necessary – in order to achieve a sufficient change in trust – to go further, and to transfer areas of pay determination entirely to worker control. Some experiments in this direction have been reported by Lawler[17].

It is notable that in his analysis of these trial innovations, Lawler uses the notion of trust as a key factor. He emphasises that when trust has been developed by participation, the effectiveness of the pay system may exceed its apparent technical limitations. In the examples he describes, there is also the striking suggestion that employees given authority for their own pay may be capable of rugged decisions which they would find it hard to tolerate if imposed by management.

An approach which I have practised recently is to use an attitude survey as a method of drawing together management and worker representatives to study pay problems jointly. A survey used for this purpose has to be of a much simpler and less formal type than those which have been described in the case-surveys of this book. Also, surveys cannot contribute effectively to innovation if they are isolated data-gathering exercises. The company has to be encouraged to set up working parties or project groups to study pay problems, in advance of, or in parallel with, the attitude survey. The latter then becomes part of a more general process of thinking about pay. A simple example concerns a manufacturing plant, where the incentive bonus scheme was particularly ill-conceived, but a management proposal to remove it had met with strong opposition. The survey revealed that most production workers considered the scheme ridiculous and would like to abolish it. A working party was set up, consisting of shop stewards and junior management, to consider the criticisms. Perhaps because they

The Problem of Authority

were helped by having a common set of information, and because of their equal position in solving the problem, the two groups were able to agree a solution relatively quickly. It must not be supposed, however, that all situations can be tackled as easily as this. The promise of using survey methods is in giving employees more influence over pay decisions, by making their opinions more apparent both to management and to worker representatives. But the new situation still has to be developed, and the conditions of trust or mistrust remain crucial. Where trust is at a low ebb, long periods of sustained effort are required to create more productive relationships. Surveys and participative working groups are merely two possible aspects of what needs to be a many-sided effort.

In any case, the preceding analysis suggests that it is not so much the technical features of the payment system which matter for conflict, as the associated processes of decision-making and control. If this is so, then improved technical design of payment systems will be ineffectual in coping with conflict. Progress will depend far more on the initiative of management and unions in making the *processes* of pay design more open to reform.

This conclusion can be either a daunting one or a hopeful one, depending upon one's opinions about the possibilities for changing organisations. It is extremely difficult to change the character of authority and power. In many organisations, it is difficult even to get such topics acknowledged, since the existence of conflicts is strenuously denied. On the other hand, there has been no shortage of ideas and innovations for introducing changes in organisational relationships. These range from large-scale developments for worker participation or co-determination in industry, to the behavioural change programmes which are referred to collectively as 'OD' (organisation development).

From a pessimistic point of view, it is true that the progress made both by participation and by 'OD' programmes has so far been relatively disappointing. But again, from a more positive point of view, the variety of approaches potentially available for pay participation or 'Pay-OD' contrasts very favourably with the limited and stereotyped range of technical ideas for pay design.

Tensions of authority and resistance to authority are deep-seated in large organisations, and the payment system is a nexus for those tensions. Can organisations innovate sufficiently to make the pay system become an area of *co-operation*? To give an unequivocal 'Yes' to such a question would be mere glibness. Methods of conceptualising, planning and measuring 'OD' programmes of any sort are in their infancy, and 'Pay-OD' must be regarded as a particularly difficult area. To have stated the necessity of facing this difficulty is, perhaps, some kind of a start. To that extent, it seems fair to claim practical relevance for the two-aspect theory of pay.

References

CHAPTER 1

1. Roethlisberger, F. J. and Dickson, W. J., *Management and the Worker* (Wiley, New York, 1939).
2. Roy, D., reported in Whyte, W. F., *Money and Motivation* (Harper & Row, New York, 1955).
3. Lupton, T., *On the Shop Floor* (Pergamon, Oxford, 1963).
4. Silver, M., 'Recent British Strike Trends: A Factual Analysis', *British Journal of Industrial Relations*, 1973, *11*, 66–104.
5. Daniel, W. W., *Wage Determination in Industry* (PEP, London, 1976).
6. Clegg, H., *The System of Industrial Relations in Great Britain* (Blackwell, Oxford, 1970).
7. Smith, C. T. B. et al., 'Strikes in Britain', *Manpower Paper No. 15* (HMSO, London, 1978).
8. Behrend, H., *Income Policy, Equity and Pay Increase Differentials*, (Scottish Academic Press, Edinburgh & London, 1973). Behrend, H., 'The Impact of Inflation on Pay Increase Expectations and Ideas of Fair Pay', *Industrial Relations Journal*, 1974, *5*, 5–10.
9. Hawkins, K., 'The Miners and Incomes Policy, 1972–1975', *Industrial Relations Journal*, 1975, *6*, 4–22.

CHAPTER 2

1. McGregor, D. M., 'The Human Side of Enterprise', *Management Review*, 1957, *46*, 22–8, 88–92.
2. Herzberg, F., 'The Motivation–Hygiene Concept and Problems of Manpower', *Personnel Administration*, 1964, *27*, 3–7.
3. Maslow, A. H., 'A Theory of Human Motivation', *Psychological Review*, 1943, *50*, 370–96.
4. Smith, P. C., Kendall, L. M. and Hulin, C. L., *The Measurement of Satisfaction in Work and Retirement*, (Rand McNally, Chicago, 1969).
5. Bartlett, F. C., *Remembering* (Cambridge, 1932).
6. Neisser, U., *Cognitive Psychology* (Appleton-Century-Crofts, New York, 1967).
7. Dulany, D. E., 'Awareness, Rules and Propositional Control: a Confrontation with S–R Behavior Theory', in Horton, D. and Dixon, T. (eds), *Verbal Behavior and S–R Behavior Theory* (Prentice-Hall, Englewood Cliffs, N. J., 1967).

8. Fishbein, M., 'The Relationships between Beliefs, Attitudes and Behavior', in Feldman, S. (ed.), *Cognitive Consistency* (Academic Press, New York, 1966). Fishbein, M., 'A Behavior Theory Approach to the Relations between Beliefs about an Object and the Attitude towards the Object', in Fishbein, M. (ed.), *Readings in Attitude Theory and Measurement* (Wiley, New York, 1967).
9. Ajzen, I., 'Attitudinal versus Normative Messages: An Investigation of the Differential Effects of Persuasive Communications on Behavior', *Sociometry*, 1971, *34*, 263–80, Fishbein, M. and Ajzen, I., 'Attitudes towards Objects as Predictors of Single and Multiple Behavioral Criteria', *Psychological Review*, 1971, *81*, 59–74.
10. Ajzen, I. and Fishbein, M., 'The Prediction of Behavioral Intentions in a Choice Situation', *Journal of Experimental Social Psychology*, 1969, *5*, 400–16.
11. Bem, D. J., 'Self-perception: an Alternative Interpretation of Cognitive Dissonance Phenomena', *Psychology Review*, 1967, *74*, 183–200.
12. Austin, J. L., *Philosophical Papers*, 2nd edn (OUP, Oxford, 1970).
13. Brayfield, A. H. and Crockett, W. H., 'Employee Attitude and Employee Performance', *Psychological Bulletin*, 1955, *52*, 396–424.
14. Vroom, V., *Work and Motivation* (Wiley, New York, 1964); Argyle, M., *The Social Psychology of Work* (Penguin Books, Harmondsworth, 1972).

CHAPTER 3

1. Weber, M., *The Theory of Social and Economic Organization* (Free Press, New York, 1947).
2. Weber, M., *ibid.* See p. 185 and elsewhere.
3. Marx, K., *Capital* (London, 1889).
4. *Report on the Development of the Social Situation in the Community in 1973*, (ECSC/EEC/EAEC Commission Report, Brussels–Luxembourg, 1974) pp. 222–3.
5. Parnes, H. S., 'The Labor Force and Labor Markets', in Heneman, H. G. *et al.*, (eds), *Employment Relations Research* (Harper & Row, New York, 1960) pp. 1–42.
6. Cothliff, J. S., *Salary Administration* (British Institute of Management, London, 1973).
7. Doeringer, P. B. and Piore, J. S., *Internal Labour Markets and Manpower Analysis* (Heath, Lexington, Mass., 1971). Kerr, C., 'The Balkanization of Labour Markets', in Bakke, E. W. (ed.), *Labor Mobility and Economic Opportunity* (MIT, Cambridge, Mass., 1954).
8. Doeringer, P. B. and Piore, J. S., *ibid.*; Brown, W. and Sisson, K., 'The Use of Comparisons in Workplace Wage Determination', *British Journal of Industrial Relations*, 1975, *13*, 23–5.
9. Beynon, H. and Blackburn, R. M., *Perceptions of Work* (Cambridge, 1972).
10. Touraine, A., *The Post-Industrial Society* (Wildwood House, London, 1974) ch. 4 (first published in French, 1969).
11. Weber, M., op. cit. See pp. 354 ff.

12. Simon, H. A., 'A Behavioural Model of Rational Choice', *Quarterly Journal of Economics*, 1955, *69*, 99–118; Simon, H. A., 'Rational Choice and the Structure of the Environment', *Psychological Review*, 1956, *63*, 129–38; Hammond, K. R. (ed.), *The Psychology of Egon Brunswik* (Holt, Rinehart, Winston, New York, 1966).
13. Festinger, L., *A Theory of Cognitive Dissonance* (Stanford University Press, Stanford, 1957).
14. Adams, J. S., 'Inequity in Social Exchange', in Berkowitz, L. (ed.), *Advances in Experimental Social Psychology*, vol. 2 (Academic Press, New York, 1965).
15. Hyman, H. H., 'The Psychology of Status', *Archives of Psychology*, 1942, *269*, 5–38 and 80–6; Hyman, H. H. and Singer, E. (eds), *Readings in Reference Group Theory and Research* (Free Press, New York, 1968).
16. Robinson, D., 'Differentials and Incomes Policy', *Industrial Relations Journal*, 1973, *4*, 4–20.
17. Blau, P. M., *Exchange and Power in Social Life* (Wiley, New York, 1964) (See ch. 4).
18. Malinowski, B., *Argonauts of the Western Pacific* (Dutton, New York, 1961): reference given by Blau, P. M., ibid. (see p. 89).
19. Robinson, D., op. cit. (see p. 7).
20. Hyman, R., 'Inequality, Ideology and Industrial Relations', *British Journal of Industrial Relations*, 1974, *12*, 171–90.
21. Behrend, H. et al., *Incomes Policy and the Individual* (Oliver & Boyd, Edinburgh, 1967); Behrend, H. et al., 'Views on Pay Increases, Fringe Benefits, and Low Pay', *Paper No. 56* (Economic and Social Research Institute, Dublin, 1970); Behrend, H. et al., 'Views on Income Differentials, and the Economic Situation', *Paper No. 57* (Economic and Social Research Institute, Dublin, 1970); Behrend, H., *Income Policy, Equity and Pay Increase Differentials* (Scottish Academic Press, Edinburgh & London, 1973).
22. Goldthorpe, J. H. et al., *The Affluent Worker: Industrial Attitudes and Behaviour* (CUP, Cambridge, 1968); *The Affluent Worker in the Class Structure* (CUP, Cambridge, 1969) (see ch. 1).
23. Huber, J. and Form, W. H., *Income and Ideology* (Free Press, New York, 1973).
24. Patchen, M., *The Choice of Wage Comparisons* (Prentice-Hall, Englewood Cliffs, N. J., 1961).
25. Jaques, E., *Equitable Payment*, 2nd edn. (Heinemann, London, 1970).
26. Cameron, S., 'Felt Fair Pay', *Department of Employment Research Paper No. 1* (HMSO, London, 1976).
27. Behrend, H., op. cit.
28. Baldamus, W., *Efficiency and Effort* (Tavistock, London, 1961).
29. Adams, J. S., op. cit.

CHAPTER 4

1. Crozier, M., *The Bureaucratic Phenomenon* (Tavistock, London, 1963).

2. Parsons, T., Introduction to: Weber, M., *The Theory of Social and Economic Organisation* (Free Press, New York, 1947).
3. Weber, op. cit., p. 248 and elsewhere.
4. Dahrendorf, R., *Class and Class Conflict in an Industrial Society* (Routledge & Kegan Paul, London, 1959).
5. The concepts used in this argument are Weber's – Weber, M., op. cit.
6. Crozier, M., op. cit.
7. Behrend, H., 'Financial Incentives as the Expression of a System of Beliefs', *British Journal of Sociology*, 1959, *10*, 137–47.
8. Roy, D., quoted in Whyte, W. F., *Money and Motivation* (Harper & Row, New York, 1955) (see p. 59 ff).

CHAPTER 5

1. Brunswik, E., 'Representative Design and Probabilistic Theory in a Functional Psychology', *Psychological Review*, 1955, *62*, 193–217.
2. Brunswik, E., 'Organismic Achievement and Environmental Probability', *Psychological Review*, 1943, *50*, 255–72.
3. Barker, R. G., 'On the Nature of the Environment', in Hammon, K. R.(ed.), *The Psychology of Egon Brunswik* (Holt, Rinehart & Winston, New York, 1966).
4. Campbell, D. T. and Stanley, J. C., *Experimental and Quasi-Experimental Designs for Research* (Rand, New York, 1966).
5. Simon, H. A., *Models of Man* (Wiley, New York, 1957).
6. Miller, G. A., Galanter, E. and Pribram, K., *Plans and the Structure of Behaviour* (Holt, New York, 1960).
7. Feigenbaum, E. A. and Feldman, J. (eds), *Computers and Thought* (McGraw-Hill, New York, 1963).
8. Cicourel, A. V., *Method and Measurement in Sociology* (Free Press, New York, 1964).
9. White, M., 'Systematic Analysis of Employee Satisfaction', Report to the Social Science Research Council (1975); 'Employment Attitudes Considered as a System with Special Reference to Pay', Doctoral Thesis, University of Lancaster (1976).
10. Hotels and Catering EDC, *Service in Hotels* (NEDO, London, 1968); *Investment in Hotels and Catering* (NEDO, London, 1969); *Why Tipping?* (NEDO, London, 1969).
11. Reiss, A. J., 'Systematic Observation of Natural Social Phenomena', Costner, H. L. (ed.), *Sociological Methodology 1971* (Jossey-Bass, London, 1971).
12. Viteles, M. S., *Motivation and Morale in Industry* (Norton, New York, 1953).
13. McClelland, D. C., 'Methods of Measuring Human Motivation', in Atkinson, I. W. (ed.), *Motives in Fantasy, Action and Society* (Van Nostrand, Princeton, 1958); Mills, C. Wright, *White Collar* (Oxford University Press, 1951).
14. March, J. G. and Simon, H. A., *Organizations* (Wiley, New York, 1957).

15. Fox, A., 'Managerial Ideology and Labour Relations', *British Journal of Industrial Relations*, 1966, *4*, 366–78; Fox, A., 'Industrial Sociology and Industrial Relations', *Research Report No. 3* (Royal Commission on Trade Unions and Employers' Associations, HMSO, London, 1966).
16. Blalock, H. M. (ed.), *Causal Models in the Social Sciences* (Macmillan, London, 1971) (see Parts IV and V).
17. Wherry, J. R. Snr, 'Underprediction from Overfitting: 45 years of Shrinkage', *Personnel Psychology*, 1975, *28*, 1–18.
18. Goodman, L. A., 'A General Model for the Analysis of Surveys', *American Journal of Sociology*, 1971, *77*, 1035–86; Plackett, R. L., *The Analysis of Categorical Data* (Griffin, London, 1974).
19. Blalock, H. M., *Causal Inference in Non-experimental Research* (University of North Carolina Press, Chapel Hill, 1964).

CHAPTER 6

1. Hotel and Catering EDC, *Manpower in the Hotel and Catering Industry* (NEDO, London, 1975).
2. Hotel and Catering EDC, *Why Tipping?* (NEDO, London, 1969).
3. Whyte, W. F., 'Human Relations in the Restaurant Industry' (McGraw-Hill, New York, 1948).
4. Hill, J. M. M., *Staff Turnover* (Hotel and Catering EDC, London, 1968).
5. Whyte, W. F., op. cit.
6. Miller, E. J. and Rice, A. K., *Systems of Organisation* (Tavistock, London, 1967).

CHAPTER 7

1. Cothliff, J. S., *Salary Administration* (British Institute of Management, London, 1973).
2. Lockwood, D., *The Black-Coated Worker* (Allen & Unwin, London, 1958).
3. Bain, G. S., *The Growth of White-Collar Unionism* (Oxford, 1970).
4. March, J. G. and Simon, H. A., *Organizations* (Wiley, New York, 1958).
5. Crozier, M., *The Bureaucratic Phenomenon* (Tavistock, London, 1963); Gouldner, A. W., *Patterns of Industrial Bureaucracy* (Routledge & Kegan Paul, London, 1955).

CHAPTER 8

1. Shimmin, S., *Payment by Results* (Staples, London, 1959).
2. Blauner, R., 'Work Satisfaction and Industrial Trends in Modern Society', in Galenson, W. and Lipset, S. (eds), *Labour and Trade Unionism* (Wiley, New York, 1960).
3. Runciman, W. G., *Relative Deprivation and Social Justice* (Routledge & Kegan Paul, London, 1966).
4. Campbell, D. T. and Fiske, D. W., 'Convergent and Discriminant Valida-

tion by the Multitrait–Multimethod Matrix', *Psychological Bulletin*, 1959, *56*, 81–105.
5. Crozier, M., *The Bureaucratic Phenomenon* (Tavistock, London, 1963).
6. Lawler, E. E., III, 'Secrecy about Management Compensation: Are there Hidden Costs?', *Organisational Behavior and Human Performance*, 1967, *2*, 182–8.
7. Shimmin, S., op. cit.
8. Commission on Industrial Relations, 'International Harvester Company of Great Britain Ltd.', *Report No. 10* (HMSO, London, 1970); 'Electrolux Ltd.', *Report No. 18* (HMSO, London, 1971).

CHAPTER 9

1. Weick, K. E., 'Middle Range Theories of Social Systems', *Behavioural Science*, 1974, *19*, 357–67.
2. Goeke, J. R., 'Some Neglected Social Indicators', *Social Indicators Research*, 1974, *1*, 85–105.
3. Simon, H. A., 'Rational Choice and the Structure of the Environment', *Psychological Review*, 1956, *63*, 129–38; Cyert, R. M. and March, J. G., *A Behavioral Theory of the Firm* (Prentice-Hall, Englewood Cliffs, 1963); Miller, J. G., *Living Systems* (Wiley, New York, 1972).
4. Festinger, L., *A Theory of Cognitive Dissonance* (Stanford, 1957).

CHAPTER 10

1. Naylor, P. D. G., 'Establishing Salary Bands', in Bowey, A. M. (ed.), *Handbook of Salary and Wage Systems* (Gower, Epping, 1975).
2. Shaw, A. G. and Pirie, D. S., 'Payment by Time Systems', in Bowey, A. M. (ed.), ibid.
3. Flanders, A., 'Measured Daywork and Collective Bargaining', *British Journal of Industrial Relations*, 1973, *11*, 368–92.
4. Gowler, D., 'Socio-Cultural Influences on the Operation of a Wage Payment System: An Exploratory Case Study', in Robinson, D. (ed.), *Local Labour Markets and Wage Structures* (Gower, London, 1970).
5. Humble, J. W., *Management by Objectives in Action* (McGraw-Hill, New York, 1970).
6. Reddin, W. J., 'Why MBO Fails', *Management in Action*, 1973, *4*, 26–7.
7. Lawler, E. E., III, 'Secrecy about Management Compensation: Are there Hidden Costs?', *Organisational Behavior and Human Performance*, 1967, *2*, 182–8.
8. Porter, L. W. and Lawler, E. E., III, *Managerial Attitudes and Performance* (Dorsey-Irwin, Homewood, Ill., 1968).
9. Younger, W. F., 'The Hay–MSL System', in Bowey, A. M. (ed.), op. cit.
10. Hawkins, K., 'The Miners and Incomes Policy, 1972–1975', *Industrial Relations Journal*, 1975, *6*, 4–22.
11. Dahrendorf, R., *Class and Class Conflict in an Industrial Society* (Routledge & Kegan Paul, London, 1959) (see pp. 267 ff).
12. Lupton, T. and Bowey, A. M., *Wages and Salaries* (Penguin, Harmondsworth, 1975).

References

13. Trist, E. L. et al., *Organizational Choice* (Tavistock, London, 1963).
14. Fox, A., *Beyond Contract: Work, Power and Trust Relations* (Faber & Faber, London, 1974).
15. Zand, D. E., 'Trust and Managerial Problem Solving', *Administrative Science Quarterly*, 1972, *17*, 229–39.
16. Cliquet, M. and Dumont, J., *Rémunération et Intéressement* (Entreprise Moderne d'Edition, Paris, 1973).
17. Lawler, E. E., III, 'Participation and Pay', Conference Paper, International Conference on Work, Pay and Performance (Amsterdam, 1974).

Index

Action
    grounded in social situation of work, 24, 39, 55–6
    relationship to satisfaction, 127–8
Adams, J. S. 37–8
Advisory Conciliation and Arbitration Service, 4
Attitudes
    different types, 17–18
    hierarchies of, 18–20, 70–1, 86, 108–9, 115–17
    motivational theories of, 13–16, 54, 124–5
    'multistructures' of, 19–20, 72, 88, 109, 117–18
    relationship to action and behaviour, 22–4, 127–8
    towards future actions, 22–4, 55
    stability of, 125–6
    towards pay, see Pay
    verbal theory of, 16–20, 124
Austin, J. L. 23
Authoritarian management, 62, 64–5, 75–6
Authority as basis of conflict, 11–12, 39–45, 83–4, 93, 96–7, 120–2, 129–30
    legitimacy of, 40
    mediated by payment systems, 43–7, 58–9, 75–6, 93, 111–13, 120–1, 129–30, 132–7

Barker, R. G. 49
Bartlett, F. C. 16
Behaviour, see Action, Verbal behaviour

Behrend, H. 6–8, 35, 45
Blau, P. M. 32
Bowey, A. M. 137
Brayfield, A. H. 23, 24
Brunswik, E. 49
Bureaucracy, 39, 41–2, 43, 79–80, 123

Calculative rationality, see Rationality
Cameron, S. 36
Campbell, D. T. 49, 108
Choice, 22–3, 55
Cliquet, M. 138
Cognitive psychology, 13, 16, 49, 125
Commission on Industrial Relations, 4, 113
'Common interests' argument, 41
Conflict
    in bureaucracy, 39–40
    necessary feature of 'imperatively coordinated' organisations, 40–1
    occurs at margin of change or uncertainty, 42–3, 77, 91–2, 97, 113
    over pay, 2–3, 11–12, 43–5, 55–6, 83–4, 93, 96, 111–14, 120–2
Criterion variables
    role in hierarchy of attitudes, 56
    selection of, 54–5, 68, 105, 114
Crockett, W. H. 23, 24
Crozier, M. 39, 41–2, 43, 45, 91, 113

Dahrendorf, R. 40–1, 42, 43, 46

Index

Daniel, W. W. 3, 6, 8, 9
Department of Employment, 5, 8
Design (of payment systems), 136–40
Differentials, *see* Pay comparisons
Dissonance theory, 31, 126–7
Documentary evidence, 51, 52, 63–4, 82
Dulany, D. E. 16–18, 24, 124
Dumont, J. 138
Economic
  explanation of conflict, 5
  rationality, *see* Rationality
  relations contrasted with social relations, 31–2
Embourgeoisement, 31
Equity
  in relation to fairness of pay, 34
  theory, 31, 37–8

Fairness, *see* Equity, Pay satisfaction
Fishbein, M. 17–19, 21, 24, 48, 124
Fiske, D. W. 108
Form, W. H. 35
Formalisation (of personnel policy), 92–4
Fox, A. 55, 137–8
'Future-attitude',
  explanation of term, 22–4
  operational definition, 55

Goldthorpe, J. H. 35
Gouldner, A. W. 93
Government intervention in pay, 135–6
Group discussion method, 51–2, 66, 102

'Hawthorne' studies, 3
Herzberg, F. 13
Hotel industry
  staff and customer relations, 62, 77
  staff terms and conditions, 62–3, 77
Huber, J. 35
Human relations school, 76–7
Hypotheses
  method of definition and testing, 57–61
  summary of findings in relation to, 115–22

Ideologies of managers and workers, 45
Incentive payment schemes, 4, 5, 45, 65, 67, 98, 100–3, 105–16
Intentions, 18, 22, 39, 55
Internal labour markets, 28–9
Interviews
  use of structured, 53, 82
  use of unstructured, 51–2, 66–7, 102

Jaques, E. 36
Job evaluation and grading, 81, 89–91, 93, 132, 136
Job satisfaction, 14, 19–22
Justice, in regard to pay, 31, 33

Labour markets
  as requirement for capitalism, 27–8
  information deficits and sources, 28–30
  internal labour markets, 28–9
Labour turnover, 63, 64, 65, 68
Lawler, E. E. 113, 138
Legitimacy of authority, 40
Lockwood, D. 83–4, 93
'Lower-level' variables
  definition of, 56
  examples of, 69, 87
Lupton, T. 3, 5, 137

McGregor, D. M. 13
Malinowski, B. 32
Management, attitudes towards, 66, 75
Management-by-objectives, 133–4
March, J. G. 55, 84–5, 93
Marx, K. 27
Maslow, A. H. 13
Measured daywork, 133
'Middle-range' variables
  definition of, 56

examples of, 69, 87
Miller, E. J. 77
Miller, G. A. 49
Motivation theories, 13–15, 54, 124–5
Multiple regression analysis, 59–60, 70–3, 86–90
Multiway contingency table analysis, 60, 74, 90, 94, 103

National Industrial Relations Court, 85
National Union of Bank Employees, 79, 85
Needs, theories of, 13–15, 19
Non-experimental methods in psychology, 49

'OD' (organisation development), 139–40
Parsons, T. 39
Participation, 138–40
Patchen, M. 35
Pay
  and authority, 11–12, 43–4, 75–6, 93, 111–12, 120–2, 129–30
  and conflict, 2–3, 11–12, 39, 43, 45–7, 75–6, 93, 96, 111–12, 120–2, 129–30
  and economic rationality, 27–30, 36–8, 74–5, 91, 110, 119–20
  and management discretion, 65–7, 75–7
  and standard of living, 66–7
  attitudes to, 26, 36–8, 39, 46–7, 58–9, 73–5, 89–91, 105–11, 116–22; hierarchy of, 73–4, 88–90, 108–9, 116–17
  comparisons, concerning differentials or relativities, 6–10, 31, 35, 73–4, 89–91; 'group-referent', 37, 90–1, 119–20; 'self-referent', 37, 90–1, 119–20
  satisfaction, 26–38, 54–5, 73–5, 89–91, 105–11, 116, 118, 121–2; equivalent to fairness of pay, 34
'Payment by results', see Incentive payment schemes
Performative utterance, 23
Power, 9, 41, 42, 45–6, 68, 76–7, 84, 92, 97, 122, 135, 137
Preferences, 22, 55
Professionalisation, 98–9

Questionnaires
  hierarchy of items, 56–7
  'self-completion' type, 53
  use of standard and non-standard items, 52–3

Rationalist theory
  of conflict, 55, 111
  of unionism, 84–5
Rationality
  calulative and economic, 27–30, 36–8, 74–5, 90–1, 110;
  underlying evaluation of pay, 36–8, 74–5, 90–1, 110
  pursuit of, by organisations, 44–5, 77–9, 81, 98–9
Reference group theory, 31
Relativities, see Pay comparisons
Rice, A. K. 77
Robinson, D. 32–3
Roy, D. 3, 45

Salaries, and job evaluation, 132–3
Salary secrecy, 134–5
Satisfaction, see also Pay satisfaction
  meaning of, 20–2
  overall, 54, 69–73, 86–8, 105–6, 108–9, 116–18; and action, 127–8
Semantics, 31–2
Shimmin, S. 104, 113
Simon, H. A. 49, 55, 84–5, 93
'Social relativism', 31–6, 74–5, 110
Status striving, 31
Strikes, 3–6, 8–9, 98, 114
Supervision, 100, 133
Surveys
  criticisms of, 48–50
  use in analysing cognitive structures, 49, 125
Systems

Index

Daniel, W. W. 3, 6, 8, 9
Department of Employment, 5, 8
Design (of payment systems), 136–40
Differentials, see Pay comparisons
Dissonance theory, 31, 126–7
Documentary evidence, 51, 52, 63–4, 82
Dulany, D. E. 16–18, 24, 124
Dumont, J. 138
Economic
  explanation of conflict, 5
  rationality, see Rationality
  relations contrasted with social relations, 31–2
Embourgeoisement, 31
Equity
  in relation to fairness of pay, 34
  theory, 31, 37–8

Fairness, see Equity, Pay satisfaction
Fishbein, M. 17–19, 21, 24, 48, 124
Fiske, D. W. 108
Form, W. H. 35
Formalisation (of personnel policy), 92–4
Fox, A. 55, 137–8
'Future-attitude',
  explanation of term, 22–4
  operational definition, 55

Goldthorpe, J. H. 35
Gouldner, A. W. 93
Government intervention in pay, 135–6
Group discussion method, 51–2, 66, 102

'Hawthorne' studies, 3
Herzberg, F. 13
Hotel industry
  staff and customer relations, 62, 77
  staff terms and conditions, 62–3, 77
Huber, J. 35
Human relations school, 76–7
Hypotheses
  method of definition and testing, 57–61
  summary of findings in relation to, 115–22

Ideologies of managers and workers, 45
Incentive payment schemes, 4, 5, 45, 65, 67, 98, 100–3, 105–16
Intentions, 18, 22, 39, 55
Internal labour markets, 28–9
Interviews
  use of structured, 53, 82
  use of unstructured, 51–2, 66–7, 102

Jaques, E. 36
Job evaluation and grading, 81, 89–91, 93, 132, 136
Job satisfaction, 14, 19–22
Justice, in regard to pay, 31, 33

Labour markets
  as requirement for capitalism, 27–8
  information deficits and sources, 28–30
  internal labour markets, 28–9
Labour turnover, 63, 64, 65, 68
Lawler, E. E. 113, 138
Legitimacy of authority, 40
Lockwood, D. 83–4, 93
'Lower-level' variables
  definition of, 56
  examples of, 69, 87
Lupton, T. 3, 5, 137

McGregor, D. M. 13
Malinowski, B. 32
Management, attitudes towards, 66, 75
Management-by-objectives, 133–4
March, J. G. 55, 84–5, 93
Marx, K. 27
Maslow, A. H. 13
Measured daywork, 133
'Middle-range' variables
  definition of, 56

examples of, 69, 87
Miller, E. J. 77
Miller, G. A. 49
Motivation theories, 13–15, 54, 124–5
Multiple regression analysis, 59–60, 70–3, 86–90
Multiway contingency table analysis, 60, 74, 90, 94, 103

National Industrial Relations Court, 85
National Union of Bank Employees, 79, 85
Needs, theories of, 13–15, 19
Non-experimental methods in psychology, 49

'OD' (organisation development), 139–40
Parsons, T. 39
Participation, 138–40
Patchen, M. 35
Pay
  and authority, 11–12, 43–4, 75–6, 93, 111–12, 120–2, 129–30
  and conflict, 2–3, 11–12, 39, 43, 45–7, 75–6, 93, 96, 111–12, 120–2, 129–30
  and economic rationality, 27–30, 36–8, 74–5, 91, 110, 119–20
  and management discretion, 65–7, 75–7
  and standard of living, 66–7
  attitudes to, 26, 36–8, 39, 46–7, 58–9, 73–5, 89–91, 105–11, 116–22; hierarchy of, 73–4, 88–90, 108–9, 116–17
  comparisons, concerning differentials or relativities, 6–10, 31, 35, 73–4, 89–91; 'group-referent', 37, 90–1, 119–20; 'self-referent', 37, 90–1, 119–20
  satisfaction, 26–38, 54–5, 73–5, 89–91, 105–11, 116, 118, 121–2; equivalent to fairness of pay, 34
'Payment by results', *see* Incentive payment schemes
Performative utterance, 23
Power, 9, 41, 42, 45–6, 68, 76–7, 84, 92, 97, 122, 135, 137
Preferences, 22, 55
Professionalisation, 98–9

Questionnaires
  hierarchy of items, 56–7
  'self-completion' type, 53
  use of standard and non-standard items, 52–3

Rationalist theory
  of conflict, 55, 111
  of unionism, 84–5
Rationality
  calulative and economic, 27–30, 36–8, 74–5, 90–1, 110; underlying evaluation of pay, 36–8, 74–5, 90–1, 110
  pursuit of, by organisations, 44–5, 77–9, 81, 98–9
Reference group theory, 31
Relativities, *see* Pay comparisons
Rice, A. K. 77
Robinson, D. 32–3
Roy, D. 3, 45

Salaries, and job evaluation, 132–3
Salary secrecy, 134–5
Satisfaction, *see also* Pay satisfaction
  meaning of, 20–2
  overall, 54, 69–73, 86–8, 105–6, 108–9, 116–18; and action, 127–8
Semantics, 31–2
Shimmin, S. 104, 113
Simon, H. A. 49, 55, 84–5, 93
'Social relativism', 31–6, 74–5, 110
Status striving, 31
Strikes, 3–6, 8–9, 98, 114
Supervision, 100, 133
Surveys
  criticisms of, 48–50
  use in analysing cognitive structures, 49, 125
Systems

of attitudes, 19, 125–7
of authority, 44–6
payment systems, *see* Pay

Taylor, F. W. 3
Tipping in hotels, 62, 64
Trust, 137–9

Uncertainty (and conflict), 42, 43, 77, 91–2, 97, 113
Understanding (of payment system), 67, 76, 102–3, 104, 111, 113, 135

Unionisation, 62–3, 98–9, 125
Unionism, white-collar, 83–5, 91–6
Union recognition, 82, 85–6

Validation, statistical, 49–50
Verbal behaviour
 dependencies as feature of, 17
 theory of, 16–17, 124

Weber, M. 27–30, 39–41, 43, 130
Whyte, W. H. 76

Zand, D. E. 137